Theology Today
The Theology of Tradition

Theology Today

GENERAL EDITOR:

EDWARD YARNOLD, S. J.

No. 11

The Theology of Tradition

BY

ANTHONY MEREDITH, S. J.

FIDES PUBLISHERS, INC.

NOTRE DAME, INDIANA

CONTENTS

ACKNOWLEDGEMENTS

The Scripture quotations are from the *Revised Standard Version of the Bible*, copyrighted 1946 and 1952 by the Division of Christian Education of the National Council of the Churches of Christ in the U.S.A. and used by kind permission. The America Press and Geoffrey Chapman, Ltd., London, have graciously given permission for quotations from *The Documents of Vatican II* (ed. W. M. Abbott, S.J.).

ABBREVIATIONS

PG: J. P. Migne, *Patrologia Graeca*

Dz: H. Denzinger & A. Schönmetzer, *Enchiridion Symbolorum Definitionum et Declarationum* (33rd edition, Barcelona etc., 1965)

7

PREFACE

No man is an island. We do not form our beliefs as so many original discoveries; we are influenced by our contemporaries and by earlier generations to a greater extent than we are sometimes prepared to admit.

Christ founded a Church which takes account of this dependence we have on one another. The Church is his Body; Christians are not so many individuals, but 'we, though many, are one body in Christ and individually members one of another' (Rom 12.5). Consequently God's revelation does not come to us principally through the written word of the Bible or the light of the Holy Spirit in the individual's mind, but by the living tradition of the whole Church as it is guided by the Spirit into all truth (Jn 16.13; cf. Matt 28.20).

Fr Meredith traces the course of the Church's growing awareness of her role of preserving this tradition and developing it as she applies it to the new situation of every age. The author shows how there has been a repeated search for a criterion by which to judge the authenticity of traditions: apostolic succession, the 'Vincentian canon', the authority of the magisterium (especially that of the pope), the *sensus fidelium* and organic growth have all been suggested. His contention is that there is no rule of thumb for identifying genuine traditions. But the Spirit cannot contradict himself; we must be sensitive to all his manifestations in Scripture, tradition, magisterium and the spiritual experience of the faithful.

E. J. Yarnold, S.J.

INTRODUCTION

The history of the way God speaks to men and calls them to belief in him begins, if we follow the Bible, with that friendly relationship sketched at the opening of the book of Genesis, when the Lord God spoke with Adam in the cool of the afternoon. It has continued since then with varying reactions on both sides. God calls in varied ways and the reply of man has varied from the obedience of faithful Abraham to the treachery of Judas. If we put this process into technical language we shall say that God makes himself and his wishes known to us in revelation and that man's response to this revelation is faith. The record of the way in which man has responded to this call is Tradition.

Tradition is the sum of the differing and interrelated responses to this impact of God upon succeeding generations of men of faith which have been handed down to us. Our main method of reaching this message of God is through the responses of others to the sound of his voice. Revelation is not merely a series of propositions or truths existing by themselves. Revelation is channelled to us through the patriarch or the prophet or the apostle or the saint, through the Church of the past or the Church of the present, and it is through these responses that we are in our turn able to understand the person of the Lord who summons us and reply in faith.

But this series of answers to the divine invitation is not simply the sum of the individual reactions to the divine call. It is rather the reply of the Church to its Lord, of the body of Christ to its head, of the people of God to the God who calls them out of darkness into his marvellous light, of the bride of Christ to her heavenly bridegroom. It is above all the reply of the spirit-filled Church to the Lord who is spirit. For that is the most important thing about the Church, as St Paul reminds us. So, writing to the Corinthians, he tells them, 'Do you not know that you are God's temple and that God's spirit dwells in you? If anyone destroys God's temple, God will destroy him. For God's temple is holy, and that temple you are' (1 Cor 3.16-17). It is the indwelling by the Holy Spirit that makes them Sons of God (Gal 4.6) and able to address the Father; it is the Holy Spirit that enables them to believe. 'Therefore I want you to understand that no one speaking by the Spirit of God ever says "Jesus be cursed" and no no one can say "Jesus is Lord" except by the Holy Spirit' (1 Cor 12.3). Prayer too is the action of the Holy Spirit within us, 'who intercedes for us with sighs too deep for words' (Rom 8.26). And finally it is the Spirit who will complete the process of revelation within each individually and in the Church. He will spell out to us the meaning of the revelation of God in Christ Jesus Our Lord.

I have yet many things to say to you, but you cannot bear them now. When the Spirit of truth comes, he will guide you into all truth; for He will not speak of his own authority, but whatever he hears he will speak, and he will declare to you the things that are to come (Jn 16.12).

It is the Spirit that acts in the Church in all its most important works and the only obstacle to the work of the Spirit is human weakness and sin. We are ever grieving the Spirit as we obstruct his work of reconciling us to the Father.

It is within this framework that we can best see the nature of Tradition. The continuous stream of understanding of Christ is the work of the Spirit as it comes to consciousness in and through the human mind. It is transmitted to us, as the recent Council tells us, in many ways, through the Holy Scriptures, the Creeds and Councils, the liturgy and devotion of the past. The action of the Spirit transcends the bounds of time and space and his action is self-consistent and unifying. To divide Christ or to deny his continued action now and in the past is to grieve the Spirit.

The following short study is an attempt to trace the way in which the Church has reflected upon her riches and her own assessment of these reflections. The method adopted is largely historical as it is felt that, although there are theological issues at stake, these can best be understood in the light of a plain account of what happened. There are obvious disadvantages in such a method, but as Tradition does not become a problem until the later Middle Ages, if then, we will be able to understand how and why it does and perhaps find some instructive parallels for a later period. The Church does not become self-conscious about her way of believing and reflecting on her beliefs until she is challenged and asked to justify the results of her own process of growing up. The first time that Tradition receives separate treatment is in the Council of Trent (Dz 1501). The fifteen hundred years that precede the Council of Trent did indeed reflect widely and fruitfully on the Christian message, but they seem to have felt little need to examine or defend their methods; they merely assume that the reflections of their predecessors, whether in Council, Creed or Scripture, do in fact introduce them to Christ. It is above all the tendency of the Reformers to identify revelation with the contents of Scripture that raises the problem of the status of the large body of Christian tradition whose links with the Bible are at times exceedingly tenuous. The question becomes less one of the contents of belief than of the reasons for it. So too, in a not dissimilar way, since the time of Descartes, the central question of philosophy has been the theory of knowledge and not the understanding of what was possessed.

CHAPTER ONE

THE PROBLEM OF TRADITION

The New Testament presents us with a picture of a man who not only promises to save us from sin but claims our total allegiance and trust as being truly God. The records of his life that have come down to us provide evidence of this claim; the fifth chapter of St John's Gospel well illustrates both the claim and the evidence in its favour. Shortly before he died he was asked by one of his earliest followers, 'Lord, show us the Father and we will be satisfied,' and Christ replies, 'He who has seen me has seen the Father' (Jn 14.8-9). Christ is the Revelation of God, and although, as the nineteenth Psalm reminds us, 'The heavens are telling the glory of God; and the firmament proclaims his handiwork', it is only in our Lord that the glory of God in creation finds its complete expression. 'He reflects the glory of God and bears the very stamp of his nature, upholding the universe by his word of power' (Heb 1.3). This is the same truth St John wishes to teach when he states at the opening of his First Epistle:

> That which was from the beginning, which we have heard, which we have seen with our eyes, which we have looked upon and touched with our hands, concerning the word of life – the life was made manifest, and we saw it, and testify to it, and proclaim to you the eternal life which was with the Father and was made manifest to us – that which we have seen and heard we proclaim also to you, so that you may have fellowship with us (1 Jn 1.1-3).

The supreme revelation of the nature of God is a person, and the response to that revelation is one of obedient

15

faith and love. Faith and love, however, both presuppose as a necessary prerequisite some degree of knowledge and familiarity. The question immediately arises, How can I find out something of the person and work of Jesus of Nazareth? How has some glimpse of his life been transmitted to me so that I may believe in him and commit myself to his care? It is on the answer to this basic question that one's attitude to the Church, tradition and redemption will turn. Who was Christ, and how do you know, and how reliable is your evidence? In framing these questions we are doing little more than repeat the question put by our Lord to the Pharisees and Sadducees when their attempts to outwit him had signally failed: 'What do you think of the Christ? Whose son is he?' (Mt 22.42). What follows in this book will be an attempt to show how this process has taken place and so to investigate what is meant by tradition.

At the outset two points of some importance should be noted. First, though it is true that the answers to our questions are of the deepest concern to many men and ought to be of the deepest concern to all men, yet the type of problem and the method of answer bear close resemblances to those asked by any historian. When he tries to discover and evaluate a figure of the past, he must find out what his sources are and endeavour to assess their reliability. He must find out the age of his manuscripts, the date at which the first copy appeared, the honesty and interest of his author and the literary form in which he is writing. Then he begins the real business of the historian which rises above the cataloguing and evaluation of evidence to the more important, if more precarious, task of interpreting the past. Interpretation implies selection and often selection implies a particular attitude to the subject in hand. Few explanations are watertight and incorrigible; further evidence may upset a long-accepted picture and compel us to alter our views.

Yet – and this is the second point – despite the similarities existing between historical inquiry and the search for Christ, we cannot apply the same tools without modification to matters of faith. The whole idea of personal relationship implicit in the notion of faith is foreign to normal historical research. It would not really make any difference now suddenly to be told that Charles I was not executed at all in 1649, but died peacefully a few years later. If, however, it could be conclusively demonstrated that the crucifixion and consequently the resurrection never happened, the effect on the lives of millions of people would be incalculable. For the important thing about Christianity is that it is an historical revelation that stands or falls upon the truth of its verifiable claims.

If the important point about faith is its historical character, the central problem of tradition concerns the way in which the divine self-revelation, the knowledge of Christ, has reached us. Can we decide the sources upon which our answer is based? There is clearly a mass of material upon which one can work; that is, there is available a large amount of evidence, documentary and otherwise, that purports to tell us something about the life and teaching of Christ. Some of this is the work of hostile critics or (rarely) of disinterested observers; but by far the bulk of what we possess comes from men who were themselves followers of Christ and consequently firmly convinced of his divinity. The most important source of information is the New Testament and within that the four gospels occupy the central position. St Paul's epistles provide relatively little by way of biographical matter, though, as we shall see later, it was not primarily biography that the evangelists intended to produce. Outside the New Testament we have evidence from early liturgies and creeds which tell us something about the way the primitive Church thought about and prayed

17

to Christ. Then again there are apocryphal gospels of Thomas, Peter and others, some of which seem to aim at filling in the gaps left in the rather stark records of the four evangelists, by supplying, for example, edifying and miraculous accounts of the infancy of Christ. Such is the material, but how far can it be trusted? Is it all of equal value? How far back does our evidence go? How near are the manuscripts we have to the date at which they were written, and how near were the writers to the events which they record? To answer these questions fully would require a good-sized book. The four main manuscripts of the New Testament we possess date to the fourth and fifth centuries, that is to within three hundred years of the date when they were written, which for ancient texts is something of an achievement: the nearest rivals are the manuscripts of Virgil. But the really difficult question is to choose the reliable sources.

It is on this fundamental question of the relative importance of the different components of the Christian heritage that the controversies surrounding the Reformation, the reply of Trent, the First and Second Vatican Councils have turned. The tendency of the Reformers and of certain groups among Catholics has been and still is to reduce the non-scriptural elements in tradition to the minor role of simply supporting the teaching of scripture; on the other hand there have been those who have talked as though scripture and tradition formed two separate sources of revelation. One would suppose that the truth lay somewhere in the middle, and such in fact is the prosaic and (to those who like quick and neat solutions) the disappointing answer at which this book, like Vatican II, arrives. This is in fact the sort of answer the Church has always given to the dilemmas with which she has been faced. So at the first Council of Constantinople in 381 she maintained that God was both one and three and at Chalcedon seventy years later she defined that

Christ was both one person and two natures. To the insistence of the heretics that it must be one *or* the other the Catholic invariably replies it is both one *and* the other. It is helpful and important to bear this in mind if one feels a vague sense of dissatisfaction at the clumsy solutions provided by the Church to the problems set her. The very fascination of heresy seems to arise from its neat coherence, and that coherence springs from its over-simplification of the data of Christianity. It would be relatively easy if one canonized a particular element in a given problem, but it often means sacrificing important parts in the process. Perhaps Christianity is not intended to be an easy religion, and perhaps it allows more scope for different emphases than its rivals like. It has been well said that had John Wesley been a Catholic he would have founded a religious order; in this way he would have expressed his God-given insight without causing any further break in Christian unity.

Tradition in its strict meaning means handing down as an active process, but before long it comes to refer to the content of what is transmitted and it is under that guise that we will come across it. But even in this secondary, derived sense it acquires a more restricted meaning still. And with the greater precision in meaning its relationship to scripture becomes more subtle and less easy to define. One of the interesting and refreshing results of the recent council has been to put the clock back and suggest that the less sophisticated state of the early Church was not without its own peculiar advantages. One word of warning is required. This book should not be read by people who are looking for neat solutions to the problems that it raises. To the real problems of life and of theology, in so far as these are separable, there are no really satisfactory verbal answers. All that may be done is to state the issue clearly and make sure that justice is done to all the important elements. If this book succeeds in convincing its readers of that, it will have fulfilled its purpose.

CHAPTER TWO

TRADITION IN THE BIBLE

> God the inspirer and author of both Testaments,
> wisely arranged that the New Testament be hidden
> in the Old and that the Old be made manifest in the
> New. For though Christ established the New Cove-
> nant in his Blood (Lk 22.20; 1 Cor 11.25), still the
> books of the Old Testament with all their parts,
> caught up into the proclamation of the New, acquire
> and show forth their full meaning in the New
> (Mt 5.17; Lk 24.27), and in turn shed light on it
> and explain it.

With these words the *Constitution on Divine Revelation*
of Vatican II ends its fourth chapter.

The Old Testament contains an account of the dealings
of God with the chosen people of Israel. It begins with
an account of creation, the first sin and the fall of man
from his state of initial happiness. From then on, it may
be seen as a record of the repeated mercies of God and
the continued returns and relapses of the Israelites. Not
that God's methods are always the same, nor is the type
of response he evokes and receives after the same pattern. There is evidence of a developing moral awareness
and more spiritual outlook at least among the prophets.
It is important to remember this historical aspect of
God's self-revelation, especially as to forget it may end
up in the two major fallacies which beset many interpretations of the Bible, allegorization and fundamen-
talism. The presupposition behind both is the same;
namely that revelation of the nature and purposes of God
is radically unhistorical and never alters. The fundamen-
talist falls into the trap of making all parts of Scripture

of equal importance and so making no effort to discriminate between, for example, the legal prescriptions of the book of Leviticus and the recorded sayings of our Lord in the Sermon on the Mount. Allegorization, on the other hand, by its ill-balanced quest for the Spirit which the letter hides, frequently uses the words of scripture as a peg on which to hang its own spiritual or philosophical systems.

The revelation enshrined in the pages of the Old Testament is itself tradition and that in two senses: it both records and interprets the past. In fact these two processes are so closely enmeshed that attempts to disentangle them are laborious and frequently meet with only partial success. The earlier chapters of Genesis, which purport to narrate the creation of the world, provide differing accounts of the same process from different angles. There is here, if you like, tradition within tradition, tradition and tradition interpreted. It will be clear that the problem of the historical Moses is of the same kind, if not of the same importance, as the problem of the 'Quest of the Historical Jesus'. For the New Testament itself is not a straight factual account of the earthly life of our Lord and Saviour; it, too, selects and to some extent interprets what it hands down.

One of its central methods of interpretation is suggested in the passage from the *Constitution on Divine Revelation* with which this chapter opens. The Old and New Testaments throw light on each other. In his book *According to the Scriptures*, C. H. Dodd has suggested that the early Church employed select portions of the Old Testament to explain for the benefit of the Jews the precise sense in which Jesus Christ was in fact the hoped-for Messiah, in whom the nation's expectations found fulfilment. A good example of this proof-text method can be seen in the seventh chapter of Acts of the Apostles, where a long apologetic defence of Christianity is put

into the mouth of St Stephen shortly before his martyr-
dom. In it he gives a brief synopsis of Israelite history,
beginning with the call of Abraham and culminating with
the nation's formal rejection of God at the Crucifixion of
our Lord, 'whom you have now betrayed and murdered'
(Acts 7.52). How, when or why this process of searching
the scriptures began is hard to say. We are fairly ac-
customed to it, but that such a remarkable feat of reinterpretation was attempted so soon after the Resurrection
does call for some explanation. The most convincing
solution is that it goes back to a tradition that begins with
our Lord himself. At his first appearance in the syna-
gogue at Nazareth,

> He stood up to read; and there was given to him the
> book of the prophet Isaiah. He opened the book and
> found the place where it is written, 'The Spirit of the
> Lord is upon me, because he has anointed me to
> preach good news to the poor. He has sent me to
> proclaim release to the captives, and recovering of
> sight to the blind, to set at liberty those who are
> oppressed, to proclaim the acceptable year of the
> Lord.' And he closed the book, and gave it back to
> the attendant, and sat down; and the eyes of all in
> the synagogue were fixed upon him. And he began
> to say to them, 'Today this scripture has been ful-
> filled in your hearing' (Lk 4.16-21).

It is very possible that this type of exegesis was both the
warrant and example for the very bold action of the early
Church. A full understanding of the message of the Old
Testament may only be found in the pages of the New.
So the author of the Epistle to the Hebrews begins his
letter to the suffering Jewish Christians as follows: 'In
many and various ways God spoke to our fathers by the
prophets; but in these last days he has spoken to us by a
Son, whom he appointed the heir of all things, through
whom also he created the world' (Heb 1.1.). This con-

viction, then, that both the natural order and the dispensation of the Old Covenant are the basis upon which a great deal of the teaching of the early apostles depends is behind the famous cosmic hymn to Christ in Colossians 1 and St Paul's remark to the Galatians that the 'law was our custodian [or pedagogue] until Christ came' (Gal 3.24).

From what has been said so far, some idea can be gained of the exceedingly elaborate process which underlies the apparently simple books of the New Testament. At the risk of over-simplification we can separate out, at least mentally, the incidents which the Old Testament purports to relate, the interpretation it puts upon them, its own reinterpretation of its earlier portions and finally the way that it itself is used as a source for understanding the Gospel of Christ.

There is, however, a further stage which can be called the New Testament theology of the New Testament. Standard works like R. Bultmann's *Theology of the New Testament*, written from a somewhat existentialist angle, and another book of the same title by J. Bonsirven from a Catholic viewpoint, draw out the implications of the primitive message of the gospel. The point is that, natural revelation and the Old Testament apart, a great deal of history already lies behind the pages of the New Testament. This is not surprising if we reflect that on any calculation the crucifixion did not occur later than 33 A.D., yet the earliest portion of the New Testament to reach the form in which we now possess it was probably the First Epistle to the Thessalonians, which did not appear until about 51 A.D. The other epistles attributed to St Paul are spread out over the next fourteen years. Most present their message from different points of view, and it is difficult to tell with any certainty whether we owe these varied approaches to the different needs of the different communities he addressed or to a development in

24

his own thought. But whichever view be taken of this problem, the fact remains that the handing down by St Paul of the message which 'I did not receive from man, nor was I taught it, but it came through a revelation of Jesus Christ' (Gal 1.12) entails a reinterpretation of the primitive tradition. He explicitly refers to a tradition behind him when he writes to the Corinthians in about 57 A.D.:

> For I delivered to you as of first importance what I also received, that Christ died for our sins, in accordance with the Scriptures, that he was buried, that he was raised on the third day in accordance with the Scriptures and that he appeared to Cephas and then to the twelve (1 Cor 15.3-5).

Earlier in the same letter (1 Cor 11.2) he exhorts them to hold fast to the traditions received, and in an earlier writing, the Second Epistle to the Thessalonians, a similar plea may be found: 'Stand firm and hold to the traditions which you were taught by us' (2 Thess 2.15). Further than this, it is generally held that the epistles embody formulas and refer to practices of considerably greater antiquity than they themselves possess. So the descriptions of the person and work of Christ at the beginning of the Epistle to the Romans and in the second chapter of the Letter to the Philippians, because of their symmetrical form, may well be transcripts of ancient hymns to Christ. Also in the references to the sacrament of baptism at Romans 6.1-11 and to the Holy Eucharist at 1 Corinthians 11.23-28 we are clearly in the presence of a tradition that goes back to the very earliest days of Christian preaching. To sum up briefly, we have in St Paul a mixture of primitive preaching and practice together with practical applications of and reflexions upon what he had learnt.

But if tradition and interpretation are present in the epistles, they are even more evident in the four gospels.

This is not the place to go into the synoptic problem and the varied traditions that lie behind the text we now possess. On the most conservative reckoning none of them reached their final forms much before 65 A.D. Further than this, it was not their author's intention to provide a simple biography of Christ. The primary purpose, as their name indicates, was to spread the good news of salvation, to which purpose the details of our Lord's life are subservient. So at the end of the Fourth Gospel St John writes: 'These things are written that you may believe that Jesus is Christ, the Son of God, and that believing you may have life in his name' (Jn 20.31). The aim in fact is to provide the sort of information that will convince the hearers of Christ's divinity, and this explains the insistence laid by SS. Luke and John on the reliability of their witness. 'It seemed to me also, having followed all things closely for some time past, to write an orderly account for you, most excellent Theophilus, that you may know the truth concerning the things of which you have been informed' (Lk 1.3). And in the Fourth Gospel on several occasions the author appeals to the authentic character of the evidence he provides (cf. Jn 1.14; 19.35).

Each of the evangelists has his own method of bringing before his readers the particular way in which Christ both fulfils and transcends the hopes and expectations of the Jews. To some extent his approach is determined by the particular audience he is addressing. St Matthew, for example, seems to have a Jewish public in mind. His gospel opens with a somewhat schematic account of our Lord's Jewish ancestry and his narrative of the birth and Infancy is couched in language full of quotations from the Old Testament. So we have: 'All this took place to fulfil what the Lord had spoken by the prophet, "Behold a virgin shall conceive and bear a son and his name shall be called Emmanuel" (which means, God with us)'

(1.22). Similar examples may be found at 2.6 and 2.18. St Luke is equally clear that Christ is the new Israel, succeeding in precisely those sorts of situation where the old Israel had failed. The temptations of our Lord are those of the chosen people in their desert wanderings, with this difference: the Jews gave way, but Christ resists. Some scholars also see in the long section that runs from Chapter 9 to Chapter 18 a deliberate attempt to follow the pattern of the book of Deuteronomy. All that passage is set between the account of the Transfiguration (9.28-36) and the triumphant entry into Jerusalem (19.28-40). It opens as follows: 'When the days drew near for him to be received up, he set his face to go to Jerusalem' (9.51). St Luke clearly intended his readers to see the journey as a prelude to the true sacrifice of the Passover. Repeated study of the four gospels reveals the many ways, some subtle, some obvious, in which both the Israelites and the individual heroes of the past have, as it were, entered into their heritage as types of the true Israel, the true Isaac and the true Moses. Finally and most clearly, Jesus is the heir to a variety of titles that sum up his mission and nature. He is the Son of Man described in the seventh chapter of the prophet Daniel; he is the Suffering Servant of the Servant songs of the Second Isaiah; he is the Messiah, Son of God and Lord. These are the main ways in which the evangelists express their conviction, drawn from their Master himself, that he was what he claimed to be.

Whatever view is taken of the extent to which the primitive teaching of Christ has been remoulded by the hands of the authors, it is impossible at this late stage to discover a satisfactory tool for separating 'objective fact' about the historical Jesus from the evangelists' editorial comments. There certainly is theology in the New Testament in so far as theology means an attempt to understand what one believes. But this theology presupposes

27

certain basic historical facts about Christ. The tradition which the Bible in both its parts presents is a complex of objective statement and interpretation. It is a mistake to suppose that handing on the truth about Christ is or ought to be like handing on a baton in a relay race, or a family heirloom from one generation to another. There is an obvious sense in which a baton and an heirloom are separate from their bearers. The truth about Christ is far more closely connected with those that hand it on.

CHAPTER THREE

TRADITION IN THE FATHERS

Reliqui vero omnes falso scientiae nomine inflati,
Scripturas quidem confitentur, interpretationes vero
convertunt. Others, however, retain the scriptures;
but are so conceited by their false knowledge that
they alter its true sense (Irenaeus, *Adv. H.*
III.12.12).

Here we are faced in this one short sentence with the two
central problems of the chapter, the content and meaning
of the New Testament. What is the New Testament and
how is it to be interpreted? For us the answer to the first
question at any rate looks simple enough. We can point
to the four gospels, the epistles of St Paul and the other
writers, to the Apocalypse and to Acts of the Apostles
and say, 'That is the New Testament'. And few will dis-
agree. But the quotation given above shows that the
position was by no means so clear to the primitive
Church.

To start with, the primary meaning of the word
'scipture' for the first writers of the Church was not the
New Testament at all but the Old Testament. So when in
56 A.D. St Paul writes to the Christians of Corinth, 'I
delivered to you as of first importance what I also received, that Christ died for our sins in accordance with
the scriptures' (1 Cor 15.3), the scriptures to which he
refers are the Old Testament. And it is only from the end
of the second century that the word 'scripture' is used to
refer to the Old and New Testaments alike. But another
reason for the uncertainty as to the contents of the New
Testament was the existence of a number of respected
writings that were quoted and used side by side with the

'real' thing. St Polycarp writing to the Philippians in Asia Minor in about 135 A.D. quotes Clement of Rome as an authoritative source for sound doctrine, alongside St Paul and the synoptic gospels. As an illustration of the general confusion surrounding a subject which to us raises few if any problems, reference may be made to a remark of Papias, a bishop of Smyrna, who lived in the first half of the second century. It is preserved for us in the *History of the Church* written by Eusebius in the first half of the fourth century.

> Papias also gives certain other things as having come down to him by unwritten tradition, and some strange parables of the Saviour and pieces of teaching, and certain other things of somewhat mythical character (*H.E.* III.39).

It does seem fairly clear from this and several other pieces of information that the neat picture of a fixed canon of the New Testament is a product of a later age. But why was the Church forced to come to the point of deciding what books she was prepared to accept as her own special books?

The answer to this and to the other question of the interpretation of the sacred books is the same, the second-century heresy of Gnosticism. The quotation with which this chapter opens speaks of men who decided either the content or the scope of scripture for themselves. The particular heretic – a word which at that time referred to various types of the gnostic menace – was Marcion. It is hard to say when and where Gnosticism began. From the very beginning of the preaching of the gospel there had not been wanting those who offered their own special brand of false understanding. It is more than likely that the adversaries attacked by St Paul in his letter to the Colossians were gnostics who laid claim to a special and occult knowledge of God. These false claims were clearly at work a few years later, as we find the following ad-

30

monition in the First Letter to Timothy: 'Avoid the god-less chatter and contradictions of what is falsely called knowledge, for by professing it some have missed the mark as regards the faith' (1 Tim 6.20).

The second century finds the gnostic heresy in a very flourishing condition. It promised salvation based on secret knowledge and escape from the toils of the flesh. In other words, it bases itself on a belief in the superiority of mind over matter or flesh and in the radical evil of matter. The physical universe is no longer seen as the image of and means towards the Lord who made it – and this is the way that the Bible sees it – but rather as a prison from which escape must be the aim of life. The moral conflict between the spirit and the flesh of which St Paul writes so passionately in the seventh chapter of the Epistle to the Romans is translated by the gnostic into a fight between body, the evil principle, and soul, the divinely-imparted and imprisoned spark. It is interesting to note that the support that the Epistle gives to this understanding of the nature of man made Romans into an unfavourable document in the second century as far as the orthodox Catholics were concerned.

This salvation that gnostics held out to the favoured souls of the second century was given by means of the secret teaching they offered which, as we have hinted, was derived either from their special sources of information or from their own interpretation of the common stock of Christian truth. Against such an attack – and it is arguably the most serious that the Church has ever been called on to face – the early Fathers of the Church had a twofold task: the establishing of the Canon of the New Testament and the attempt to discover some criterion whereby to decide which were the true and which the false understandings of the evidence. But what is the criterion for deciding between authentic and inauthentic interpretation and authentic and inauthentic scripture?

How was the Church to refute the claim advanced by the Montanists that the Holy Spirit had spoken through their prophets in a better way than he had done through the original apostles? For the solution of both of these problems the appeal is made over the heads of the heretics to the teaching and authority of the apostles. So Dr S. L. Greenslade well observes,

> To the Gnostics who boasted either to have discovered new truth or to possess secret tradition and to the Montanists who believed that the revelation to and through the Apostles had been surpassed by the Paraclete's particular inspiration of their own prophets, the Church declared that it stood by the Apostolic teaching, summed up in the Apostolic rule of faith and in general by the tradition of the Church as founded by the Apostles (*Schism in the Early Church*, p. 169).

The immediate and important question for the Church to come to a decision about was this: what were the books that possessed apostolic authority and what were the truths to which the apostles had given their assent? It is difficult to know at what date the Church made up its mind to erect apostolicity as the criterion for the canon of scripture, but by about the year 200 the Bishop of Rome had made up his mind, and the result is to be found in the Muratorian Canon which lists the books that are to be accepted. Apart from the omission of the Epistle to the Hebrews as a non-apostolic production, it reads very much like the contents of our New Testaments. So much for the attempt of the gnostic Marcion to tailor the Bible to meet his own requirements and omit the whole of the Old Testament and most of the New from his list of desired reading. He had left only the Epistles of St Paul and an edited version of the Third Gospel.

The problem of the understanding of the Christian

32

message and of the New Testament in particular is rather more tricky. As we have already seen, *gnosis* can also mean the deep underlying sense of scripture, and it is at this that any real attempt to understand the message of Christ must aim. Unfortunately there is no easy clue to the sense of scripture. Interpretation depends on the selection of the relevant or seemingly relevant facts, and there is no guarantee that all men will select in the same way. The case made out against the heretics rests on the teaching of the Church that goes back to the apostles. Such an approach can be found in several places. St Irenaeus, Bishop of Lyons in the latter half of the second century, produced his refutation of the gnostics in a five-volume work called *Adversus Haereses*. At the beginning of the third book he writes, 'When *we* appeal to that tradition which is kept by the successive elders in the churches, *they* oppose that tradition and lay claim to a wisdom superior to that of both elders and apostles.' And a little further on in the same book: 'This tradition may be seen by all who would do so in every church, some of which trace their origins as far back as the apostles themselves.' Irenaeus then quotes the list of the bishops of Rome as being good examples of the point he wishes to make. You can establish true doctrine by appealing to the teaching of those who have the closest links with those authors and eyewitnesses of the faith, the apostles. Here is something every man can inspect and measure himself by. It is not some secret mysterious teaching to which not even the apostles had access.

The exact nature of the test to which St Irenaeus appeals is not totally clear and has provoked some discussion. Is it a rule of faith, i.e. a formula which is an infant version of the Creed, or is it simply a way of interpreting the New Testament? In other words, what is the relationship between the standard to which he appeals and the Word of God as it is offered to us in holy

33

scripture? Is scripture to be understood by the deep penetration of which the Greek Fathers are so fond or is there some external criterion independent of the Bible itself? To put the question in a slightly different way: what is the relationship between the Word of God and the rule of faith? On this point St Irenaeus is ambiguous. He simply appeals to the authority and teaching of the apostolic age without specifying the connections that are to be found among the various elements that go to the making of Catholic truth.

Tertullian, who wrote at the opening of the third century, is more explicit on the subject. In about 206 he produced the *De Praescriptione Haereticorum* (the heretics are still gnostics), in which he rejected any oversimplified doctrine of the *Scriptura sola* (Scripture alone) variety. Scripture, he rightly maintains, does not provide its readers with a clue to its own meaning. There must be some standard or criterion external to itself to judge by. What is this criterion? In Chapter 13, in answer to the question, 'Where is the truth to be found?', after denying that the heretics possess it, he claims,

Our rule of faith: ...There is one God and no other, who created the earth and produced everything out of nothing by his word, sent forth before all things. The same word spoke through the prophets, was called on by patriarchs and finally was made man in the womb of the Virgin Mary.

This is surely a primitive version of the creed or rule of faith. But, as with Irenaeus, so here also it is hard to determine with any accuracy the relation between it and the scripture it is to help interpret. Although it is not an exact replica of any one passage in the canon, it is full of phrases from and echoes of the New Testament. It has not yet reached the full grandeur of the Creed of the Council of Constantinople of 381, which in places has no very clear link with the Bible. Even so it bears witness to

34

an attempt to condense the message of the gospel into a simple form to which a man could easily give assent when the moment for baptism came.

The search for the meaning of the message of the gospel, for the mystery of Christ, takes various forms of which several have already passed under review. The canon has been established, the creed is beginning to be thought of as the standard of orthodoxy and in addition to these two important developments we can also catch a glimpse of the authority of the bishop, as well as of the past, determining belief. What was the source in the Church *now* which could provide the faithful with the answers to the many perplexities with which the infant body was faced? If the teachings and writings and traditions of the apostles were of such paramount importance in the fight with the gnostic, where did the authority of the apostles now reside? As early as the beginning of the second century we find St Ignatius of Antioch talking of the bishop as God's viceroy upon earth to whom as to the apostles attention must be paid. And if you are looking for anything more specific than that, Irenaeus appeals to those churches which owe their foundation to the apostles, Rome or Antioch or Ephesus (*Adv. H.* III.3). The argument seems to be that the contemporary bishop of Rome or Ephesus is a lineal descendant of St Peter or St John and enjoys the same sort of prestige as his illustrious predecessors. This meant that the Church did not have to depend in its ministry of the word on what it could reconstruct of the teaching of the apostles, as here was the voice of the apostles among them. A further consequence of the authority of the bishop was to stress the public corporate nature of the doctrine of the Church and so to do away with the odious distinctions between true initiated Christians and also-rans that the gnostic system gave rise to. You did not and you do not have to belong to a particular set or be particularly clever to be a good Christian. Though it must be admitted that two of the most illustrious members of the Alexandrian church by the very way they discuss the faith leave themselves wide open to the charge that they believe there are two classes of believers, the simple faithful and the *cognoscenti* or the *illuminati*.

Side by side with the gradual establishment of the canon and the search for a principle of interpretation, we are faced with the actual attempts on the part of the Fathers of the Church to penetrate the central mystery of the faith. Scripture is the basis from which all of them start, and a large amount of the remains of Christian antiquity is made up of the commentaries or sermons of the Fathers on the books of the Bible. The second century is the age of the Apologists of the Church, men of the calibre of Justin (died c. 154) and Irenaeus (d. c. 202). But with the growth in the numbers of the faithful and the gradual decline in the persecution of the Church and of the need to provide a philosophical defence against the criticism of the heathen, the scholars and bishops were able to turn to the more fruitful task of interpreting the faith for the benefit of the believers. The bulk of Origen's writing (d. 253) consists of lengthy comment on the Bible; an enormous commentary on the Fourth Gospel survives, though in a reduced state, and most of the Old Testament is dealt with by him. Then there is the massive exegetical production of St John Chrysostom (d. 407), which is concerned almost exclusively with the New Testament. The methods of the two differ, as they are representatives of the two main schools of exegesis, the allegorizing school of Alexandria, and its counterpart in Antioch that insisted on more literal interpretation; but the aim is the same, that they may introduce their hearers into 'all the riches of assured understanding and the knowledge of God's mystery, of Christ, in whom are hid all the treasures of wisdom and knowledge' (Col 2.1-3).

But despite, or perhaps because of, all this activity, people had been growing more aware of the drawbacks to the previous answers to the question about the source of authority in matters of doctrine in the Church. Although the attack from the hostile world of paganism was at least officially at an end, it could not escape the observant that matters of doctrine were not easily solved. The Arian controversy fragmented the Church for over sixty years, and it was hard for anyone to say who would win in the end or what was the right answer to the problem. It was easy enough for the turbulent Jerome writing well after the Council of Sirmium to say that at that juncture the world had been astonished and pained to see itself become Arian, but how was it possible to tell in the actual situation? There was no universally recognized centre of authority in the present, and the past could scarcely be expected to answer the sort of questions it had never dreamed of asking. St Augustine in a well known phrase had proposed an answer to the problem in a letter to Parmenias: '*Securus iudicat orbis terrarum* – the verdict of the world is decisive.' But as an answer to the problem of how to decide between conflicting traditions that is but a paper solution. If all the world agrees on a point there is very little call for a general decision. Much the same sort of objection may be raised to the answer provided by Vincent of Lerins in the fifth century. It runs quite simply: '*Quod semper quod ubique quod ab omnibus:* that is to be believed which has been held by everyone always everywhere.' But despite the epigrammatic character of this utterance it leaves much to be asked, as there are very few, if any, Christian truths of which it is true. One has only to glance at the gradual growth of the doctrine of the Holy Spirit to realize the inadequate nature of this formula as a means to deciding whether or not some as yet disputed article of faith is to be

37

believed. If the Vincentian Canon is true, it makes the growth of Christian doctrine very hard to account for.

The age of the Fathers, then, shows signs of already having arrived at the important stage of being aware of and trying to offer a solution to the central problem of this book: How can one know with certainty the true meaning of Christ? In the interest of preserving sound doctrine against the onslaughts of heretics and for the edification of the faithful, the patristic age established the canon of the New Testament and provided its own elaborate and often learned commentaries on the Word of God, which themselves as time went on came to be treated as authoritative; and it defined the orthodox and Catholic sense of the gospel at the great ecumenical Councils of Nicaea (325), Constantinople (381), Ephesus (431) and Chalcedon (451). But its attempts to provide a rule of thumb for breaking through the *impasse* reached when tradition conflicted with tradition we have glanced at and regrettably found wanting. Still, if the problem of tradition versus scripture does not yet receive the firm outlines that subsequent generations were to try to foist upon it, that was because the Fathers had not yet lost that whole sense of both tradition and gospel which draws the two closer together and which we today are trying to recapture. Similarly the connected problem of the function and nature of authority in the Church had yet to be seriously tackled. Perhaps the most important lesson, however, the age has to teach us is that what the writings of the Fathers, the decrees of general councils and the liturgy contain is not to be thought of as scraps of unscriptural information, but rather aspects of the saving mystery at least implied by the scriptures. This was, as we shall see, the position adopted by the Second Vatican Council, which is in many ways a return to the age of the Fathers.

CHAPTER FOUR

AUTHORITY IN THE CHURCH

From what has already been said it will be evident that the nature and exercise of authority in the Church is one of the crucial issues in any theology of tradition. Particularly now since the publication of the encyclical *Humanae Vitae*, the relation of individual conscience to the voice of the official magisterium has become a matter of both urgency and confusion. The problem is frequently expressed in such questions as: Has authority any rights over against individual freedom? Or, more theologically: Has the Church the unrestricted right to interpret the voice of the Bible and tradition? Can the Church lay down moral precepts that all her members must obey, and may it change the moral precepts that it has already laid down in the past?

It may help us in our investigation of authority in the Church if we consider its scope in civil life. The *Oxford English Dictionary* defines authority in general as 'the power or right to enforce obedience; moral or legal supremacy; the right to command or give an ultimate decision'. It is difficult to see how any society or group of men could long continue to exist with any degree of success unless some principle of authority were accepted among them. Although it is true that the particular form which the authority assumes will differ from century to century and from place to place, even so the general purpose remains the same, the peace and prosperity of the society in question. So if the society exists primarily to preserve and promote the interests of those in power, the form of government will differ noticeably from that of one which serves the greatest advantage of the greatest number. A slave-society, a feudal society and a democratic society do not pursue the end proposed in the same way. But whatever be the individual divergences, all are forced if they wish to survive to invoke some order and authority for the good of all interests. Even the most liberal theories of society admit the right of the state to curtail the exercise of individual freedom in the interest of the public welfare. Authority is for the public good; it is a means to an end.

Civil society can only legislate for the external behaviour of citizens, leaving their consciences, motives and beliefs to look after themselves. Even in the sphere of behaviour the area of liberty accorded to private persons is large, though the extent to which individuals are left free to pursue their private advantage will differ according to the type of government in power at the time. A socialist state will be more protective of the weaker elements than an old-fashioned liberal society. Today, as society becomes more permissive, the extent to which the state may interfere in the ordering of private lives is hotly disputed. In England, the recent dispute over the relaxation of the laws prohibiting abortion or homosexuality between consenting adults illustrates the difficulty of drawing a line between what is of public concern and what is not. Is the state the guardian of public morality or is it merely the maintainer of some minimal standard of observable behaviour?

With the model of authority in the state in mind, we may now turn to the Church and ask whether authority must necessarily belong to the Church, and if so whether it has the same meaning and extent as civil authority. Authority of some sort there must be. Its authority indeed must be wider than the authority of the state, for it claims a deeper allegiance, and claims the right to influence not only external conduct but even the most hidden thoughts and motives. Now authority in the private sphere may be no more than an inherent quality that commands respect. But the Church's authority must be more than this; like the authority of the state, it includes the power to command. For the Church is not, as some would claim, an unseen, purely internal realm, where the soul may meet its Maker in complete privacy. It is a structured society, the body of Christ bound together by professing the same doctrines, accepting the same moral rules and having the same sacraments. It is at the same time an invisible and a visible society, united by the conviction that God revealed himself at a particular time in Palestine in a particular person, Jesus Christ. If this person really has proposed certain beliefs and ways of acting as the true path of salvation for mankind, it cannot be a matter of minor importance that these teachings should be accurately known. It is the function of authority in the Church to make sure that this precious message is neither lost nor tampered with. Authority, then, serves the general good of the Church by preserving the means of redemption. It exists for the spiritual good of the people of God. It may not arbitrarily tamper with the deposit of revelation, nor ought it to be eager to dispense with unfashionable articles of faith and substitute popular ones in their place. Religious or ecclesiastical authority is 'mainly a power to influence belief or conduct' (*The Oxford Dictionary of the Christian Church*, p. 111).

But it does not follow from what has been said that the authority that the Church wields is the same kind of power as that which is exercised by the state. There have been periods in the Church's history when the Pope has been regarded as the supreme secular power in the world who possessed powers of overlordship over other rulers. Although the Pope still exercises sovereignty over his tiny Vatican state, no one now seriously believes that civic authority is an essential right of the Church. The more subtle danger in this regard is the Church's recurrent temptation to ally itself to the ruling party of the time. In this way the Church, seeking temporal power for the sake of freedom to pursue its spiritual goal, can become the champion of privilege against the rights of the poor. Again, on many occasions, the Church has felt justified in seeking the support of the 'secular arm' in order to curtail the activities of heretics, or even to coerce them into joining the Church. Happily, this last form of worldly authority can no longer be practised in good faith, now that Vatican II has declared that 'in matters religious no one is to be forced to act in a manner contrary to his own beliefs' (*Declaration on Religious Freedom*, 2).

Undoubtedly our Lord's own exercise of authority is the best indication of its true character within the Church. According to the Fourth Gospel Christ's own authority derives from his relationship to and dependence upon the Father.

> Truly, truly, I say to you, the Son can do nothing of his own accord but only what he sees the Father doing; for whatever he does that the Son does... For as the Father raises the dead and gives them life, so also the Son gives life to whom he wills (Jn 5.19-21).

Christ's obedience to the Father's will is the source of his strength. So he says, 'My food is to do the will of him who sent me and accomplish his work' (Jn 4.34). His consequent power and authority in speaking of moral matters was clear to his audience. 'He taught them as one having authority, and not as their scribes' (Mt 7.29). Again, to the soldiers who came to arrest him in the garden beyond the brook Kidron the force of his personality seems to have been evident. 'When he said to them, "I am he", they drew back and fell to the ground' (Jn 18.6). There is here no crude assertion of power of the type he was tempted to employ during his temptations in the wilderness. The power is certainly there, but not its abuse for personal aggrandizement. In reply to Peter's generous but brash attempt to save his Master by cutting off the ear of the servant of the High Priest, our Lord says, 'Do you think that I cannot appeal to my Father and he will at once send me more than ten legions of angels?' (Mt 26.53). Power is there but is kept in reserve, and humility is his principle of behaviour. Such too is the pattern he proposes for his disciples. On the one hand he gives them great power and honour in his kingdom: 'You are those who have continued with me in my trials; as my Father appointed a kingdom for me, so do I appoint for you' (Lk 22.28-29). But on the other hand he gives quite clear instructions on the way he wishes them to exercise this power. His own behaviour is set before them as a model:

> You know how those who are supposed to rule over the gentiles lord it over them and their great men exercise authority over them. But it shall not be so among you; but whoever would be great among you must be your servant, and whoever would be first among you must be slave of all. For the Son of man also came not to be served but to serve, and to give his life as a ransom for many (Mk 10.42-45).

The washing of the feet in the thirteenth chapter of St John serves his chosen apostles as an acted parable of their service as teachers of the gospel. But this *diakonia*, this service of the Word of which St Paul has so much to say, is not meant to be an irresponsible abdication of the duty to preach the gospel in season and out of season. Nor does service imply a weak surrender to all forms of private demands.

When the gospels speak of our Lord's authority (*exousia*), they mean moral authority, i.e. the power to persuade that is possessed by a man who has won trust by his competence, rather than some form of political authority, i.e. the right to coerce. He did not hesitate to

43

command, but did not use physical power to reinforce his moral authority. However, as early as the Epistles of St Paul, we see the Church assured of its right to use coercion. A Christian found guilty of incest must be expelled from the community (1 Cor 5.2). We can see the bishops exercising the right to govern the local Church as early as the beginning of the second century in the letters of St Ignatius of Antioch. The Church therefore very soon began to develop a structure and an external form of government which derived from Christ both its warrant and some of its distinctive features. This development was inevitable and right. All the same, the different grades in the Church's hierarchy must exercise their institutional authority in the same spirit of humble service with which our Lord exercised his charismatic leadership.

It has been said that the Church's authority consists mainly in the power to influence belief or conduct. Yet nowadays, both inside the Church and outside, there exists a common conviction that the formation of conscience and the pattern of belief are both individual matters. Here one is brought to the heart of the contemporary problem of authority. If each person can and ought to decide for himself what he will do and say and believe, in what possible way can the Church exercise the lordship it claims over such individual concerns? One way of meeting the problem – and it is still to be found in certain episcopal statements – is to say that the teaching of the Church must always prevail over the individual's personal judgments. Since the latter can always be obscured by prejudice, the most prudent course of action, it is suggested, is always to follow the teaching of the Church, whatever one's private convictions. The decision to become or to remain a Catholic entails the belief that the Holy Spirit guides the Church in its teaching, and the obligation to obey this teaching. Christ s the Way (Jn 14.6), and we can learn this Way most surely through the teaching of the Church. This unquestioning acceptance of the Church's teaching makes life a good deal easier; though it can result in a certain degree of immaturity. Nowadays, however, the Church has begun to pay more attention to the fact that the hierarchy, i.e. those members of the Church who have been entrusted with authority to teach, do not possess a monopoly of the Holy Spirit's guidance. The Holy Spirit also guides all the faithful.

> The Holy People of God shares also in Christ's prophetic office... The body of the faithful as a whole, anointed as they are by the Holy One (cf. Jn 2.20, 27), cannot err in matters of belief. Thanks to a supernatural sense of the faith which characterises the People as a whole, it manifests this unerring quality when, 'from the bishops down to the least member of the laity' (St Augustine, *De Praedestinatione Sanctorum*, 14, 27), it shows universal agreement in matters of faith and morals (*Dogmatic Constitution on the Church*, 12).

Indeed, some would say that the guidance that the Holy Spirit gives to the magisterium is only a particular instance of the general guidance that the Holy Spirit gives to the whole Church. In theory, according to this view, there can be no clash between the voice of the Spirit speaking through authority and his voice as he speaks in the hearts and minds of the faithful (*sensus fidelium*). In such circumstances the voice of religious authority, instead of enjoying an unchallenged control over the minds of Catholics, becomes simply one of two voices that call for a hearing.

If either authority or the individual judgment is raised to a dominating position to the exclusion of the other, licence or anarchy on the one hand or legalism and tyranny on the other can easily follow. There is no neat, rule-of-thumb solution to the problem; when there is a clash between one's own conclusions and those of the magisterium, the truth can only be found by supernatural means, faith, obedience, wisdom and the search for God's will in prayer. Of one thing we can be certain. The Holy Spirit can never drive any one to abandon the Church, for the Church, imperfect though she is, is our only source of the Spirit.

To forget or seriously to underplay either of these factors is to abdicate part of one's following of our Lord. Either extreme is in a sense easy, though the results can be tragic. To overstress the obedience of the subject and the enlightenment of the superior is to open the doors to an unchristian despotism; to overstress the freedom of the subject and the superior's duty to serve is to run the risk of losing the enlightening and unifying guidance of the Spirit as he speaks through the magisterium. And although it is quite true, as St Augustine at one time thought, *non est religionis cogere religionem* (it is not the business of religion to enforce itself), yet religion lived with the desire to create rather than discover the holy will of God may well turn into a disguised form of humanism.

CHAPTER FIVE

TRENT AND AFTER

The stage on which the Council of Trent (1545-63) was acted out was the Protestant Reformation of Luther and Calvin. And in its turn the Reformation can be understood only in connection with the Church as it existed in the late fifteenth and early sixteenth centuries. There are several features of the Church of the period which help to make the revolt against it easier to understand. The current philosophy, a debased form of scholasticism, was incapable of providing any particularly enriching form of spiritual life. Not only was the official theology of the Church, whether Thomist or nominalist, arid. Its authority, and with it that of the official Church, was weakened both by the new learning and new confidence of the renaissance and by the attacks made by humanist writers like Erasmus upon the arguments and presuppositions of the Schoolmen. In such a situation any attempt to silence the voice of free criticism by the usual methods was scarcely likely to be successful. Western spirituality had in places tended to be divorced both from scripture and theology. The most famous passage in this connexion comes from the *Imitation of Christ*. 'What is the advantage of high thoughts about the Trinity, if you lack humility and are thereby displeasing to the Trinity?' And again, 'I had rather feel compunction than know its definition' (I.i.3). This tradition had developed alongside a conviction among the superstitious that salvation could be earned and religion practised by the 'complexities and irrationalities of popular devotion'.

Together with this divorce between external and internal there was, as is well known, much corruption in the official Church. The moral waywardness of many of

47

the higher clergy, the extravagance and worse of the Roman court, glaring abuses like the possession by one bishop of several sees and Luther's *bête noire*, the sale of indulgences, combined to present a sorry picture to anyone with high ideals of what the bride of Christ should look like. True, there was a reforming party in the Church at the opening of the century, but there was only one pope in the first quarter of the century, Adrian VI, who took the matter at all seriously, and his pontificate lasted only a year, 1522-23. Finally, to complete the picture, the prestige of the papacy was at a low ebb. The Babylonian captivity of the popes at Avignon, followed by the Great Schism, had greatly enfeebled the moral force of the successor of St Peter. This weakening process was furthered by the Council of Constance (1415-18) and the Conciliar Movement, that elevated the authority of the council over that of the Pope. Nor had the personal morals and ambitions of the renaissance popes much helped to mend the situation. Julius II (1503-13) and Leo X (1513-21) looked more like colourful and cultivated princes than shepherds of the flock of Christ's Church. It must have been hard to keep a sense of proportion at such a time, and this gave further cause for more spiritual men to retire from any active part in the life of the Church.

Mention must also be made at this point of the Conciliar Movement. The misfortunes of the papacy had raised in an acute form the question of the proper relationship between the pope and a general council. It had even been suggested by men like John Wyclif that bad popes need not be obeyed and that a general council was superior to the pope and could judge and depose unsuitable ones. Considerable force was lent to such claims by the fact that the Council of Constance did in fact terminate the Great Schism, and the conciliar movement gained ground as a result.

Luther's aim was partly to free the Word of God from the trappings with which he saw it, as he thought, enmeshed. It was in danger of being totally suffocated by the rank, impure growth of mediaeval piety and doctrine. But not only had the central teaching of the gospel been obscured; the solely sufficient function of Christ had given place to the cult of our Lady and the saints; the doctrine of works and sacraments had overshadowed the central position of faith. According to Luther, the Catholic system of his day was in flat contradiction to the teaching of St Paul, especially as it finds expression in the Epistles to the Romans and the Galatians. In these, his favourite works, Luther discovered that man is justified by faith in Christ and not by the works of the law. 'Now the righteousness of God has been manifested apart from the law, although the law and prophets bear witness to it, the righteousness of God through faith in Jesus Christ for all who believe' (Rom 3.21-22). Such a doctrine helps to establish the sovereignty of God and the sole mediatorship of Christ. 'There is one God, and there is one mediator between God and men, the man Christ Jesus' (1 Tim 2.5).

Together with this emphasis on faith alone we find the sister doctrine of *scriptura sola* (scripture alone), the challenge of the Reformers to the tradition-encrusted Church they had grown up with. Although it is true that Luther opposes gospel and law, for him gospel has not the wide-embracing sense we find in St Paul.

I am astonished that you are so quickly deserting him who called you in the grace of Christ and turning to a different gospel – not that there is another gospel, but there are some who trouble you and want to pervert the gospel of Christ (Gal 1.6-7).

Here 'gospel' cannot mean the written word of scripture, but the total message of redemption in Christ. He is the content of the gospel both inside and outside the text.

49

The major drawback of the Reformers was precisely this, that by narrowing down the sense of the word 'gospel' they compelled others to do the same. Luther chose the terms in which the fight was to be waged and the Council of Trent was forced in her reply to adopt the distinction between scripture and tradition, much to the disadvantage of subsequent thought. Thanks to the impulse provided by Luther, an appearance of precision was introduced into the debate, which was foreign to the patristic period and which, as we shall see, Vatican II in its *Decree on Divine Revelation* has endeavoured to do away with. But whether it is at all possible to do away with the distinctions of the past, however misguided, is at least an open question.

One of the main advantages of Luther's position is that it appears to provide a tidy answer to the difficulties it faces. But despite its simple appearance, we should not be beguiled. Neither Luther nor Calvin was consistent in abiding by his own doctrine. Scripture does not point straight at the dogma of the Trinity, yet when a lapsed monk denied the doctrine, Calvin had him burnt for heresy at Geneva. Luther too had little sympathy with the Anabaptists, who might well have claimed that they were only carrying his own principles to their logical conclusion in their refusal to allow infant baptism. In fact, when it came to the rub, the Reformers were in many respects no less authoritarian in their attitude to scripture than the Church they had left. They had indeed shorn away many devotions and beliefs that had sprung up in the Church on the grounds that they were unscriptural, but before long an increasing arbitrariness appeared; the councils of the first five centuries might be accepted, but (ominously) the Books of Maccabees were rejected as uncanonical and the Epistle of St James was pronounced an 'epistle of straw'.

Trent was forced to answer the challenge of the Re-

formers in their own language; but to the simple either-
or of Protestantism the Church replied with a not so
simple both-and. Thus, we are saved neither by works
alone nor by faith alone but by faith and works. The
same approach appears in the decree on scripture and
tradition which was passed at the fourth session of the
Council of Trent on 8 April 1546. Scripture alone is not
sufficient; tradition also brings the gospel teaching.

This decree was the origin of the later theory that
there are two sources of revelation: scripture and tradition. In fact, although the decree set the fashion by
adopting these terms, the doctrine it expresses by them
is somewhat different from the later 'two-source' theory.

First, the decree does not say that *revelation* is to be
found in scripture and tradition, but that 'the truth and
discipline' of the gospel are to be found there (Dz 1501).
Now by 'discipline' the Fathers seem to have meant
principles of action going back to apostolic times, both
moral principles and disciplinary or liturgical regulations,
like St Paul's insistence that women should cover their
heads in church. The scope of 'truth and discipline',
therefore, is wider than the traditional meaning of 'revelation'.

Secondly, though the document uses the word 'source'
in connection with scripture and tradition, it speaks of
the gospel (in the broad sense) as the source (i.e. origin)
of truth and discipline, not of scripture and tradition as
sources (i.e. media) of revelation.

Thirdly, a change was made in the text of the passage
in question. Before revision it read, 'This truth and discipline [of the gospel] is contained partly in written
books, partly in unwritten traditions'. In the final version,
however, the 'partly... partly' of the original has been
replaced by 'both... and', so that it reads, 'This truth and
discipline is contained both in written books and in unwritten traditions'. J. R. Geiselmann maintains that the

51

change is significant and points to a desire on the part of the Fathers of Trent not to separate out the two elements of which the picture is composed. Several Fathers had expressed strong objections to the original wording which seemed to imply that tradition held an equal status with scripture and that the Bible did not contain the whole of the gospel message. It would have been characteristic of the procedure followed at Trent if a formula had been chosen which succeeded in condemning the heretics without denying a view held by a substantial party within the Church. The final version of the decree would on this interpretation have rejected *scriptura sola* while refraining from defining the connection between scripture and tradition. However, it is possible that Geiselmann is reading too much into the substitution of 'both... and' for 'partly... partly'. It was made at the last moment and apparently aroused no comment, although the Fathers had persistently refused to make another alteration designed to allay the misgivings of those who thought the wording of the decree implied that traditions were as important as scripture.

Be that as it may, it is evident that this Tridentine decree is a rejection of the Lutheran *scriptura sola*. But after the close of the Council in 1563, a hardening of the mental arteries took place and a form of the two-source theory became accepted as the orthodox teaching of the Church. Protestantism was popularly thought of as the religion of the Book; Catholicism as the religion of authority and tradition. Both pictures are inadequate caricatures but were of great use in matters of controversy and for purposes of identification. But the really important issue at stake in the whole business is the role of authority.

In his book *The Nature of Tradition*, the German theologian Joseph Ratzinger argues that the problem of the sufficiency of scripture is secondary to that of the abuse of authority. What is there to measure the pronouncements of the magisterium of the Church? Who will keep an eye on the policeman? If the Church and the Bible appear to be in conflict, which ought to be followed? It is all very well to claim that there can be no real conflict between them if both are authentic expressions of the voice of God; but that is precisely the problem, how can one know which is authentic? We are up against the same difficulty as at the end of the last chapter.

As has already been hinted, the Reformers, despite all the apparent clarity of their protest, were not slow to discover that they could not dispense with extra-scriptural material with quite the same free abandon as they had once supposed. The first four ecumenical councils of the Church were accepted as authentic interpretations of the Word of God in Scripture. But despite their capitulations on this front, there was no real rapprochement with the Catholics, whose reliance on tradition in its narrower sense made their adversaries afraid that they were still at their old tricks of depriving the Word of God of its power to operate directly upon the souls of men. Behind the different positions there were two interestingly contrasted ways of looking at authority and tradition. For a Catholic, they acted as a hedge or shield to prevent the Word of God losing any of its fulness with the progress of time; for the Protestant, however, they were a block or obstacle preventing man from approaching his Creator and Redeemer face to face. Similarly, the Protestant depreciated any reference to the efforts a man may make in his journey to salvation. For him there was no sense in which a man merited his eternal reward; to God alone belonged the credit; and to claim any merit for our own efforts was to usurp what belonged by right to God only. '*Soli Deo gloria* – to God alone be the glory'. The Catholic reply was that one's salvation was both God's work and one's own. As God's self-revelation is not to be found in scripture alone, so man's salvation is not the work of God alone, effected without the co-operation of man. We were indeed redeemed by the suffering and death of Christ on the cross, but this process is not complete unless we appropriate for ourselves the saving merits of Christ.

The same thread seems to run through the whole of the theology of the Reformers. In their anxiety to preserve the sovereignty and complete freedom of God from all human ways of acting they produced a doctrine of revelation and redemption that denied to corrupt human nature all power to co-operate. The only thing a man whose intellect and will are stained by sin can do in the presence of the blinding holiness of God is to admit his sinfulness and accept an unconditional and undeserved gift, and pass on untouched the good news he has received to others.

In practice the thorough-going Protestant system does not work. Its belief in the supreme importance of private judgment did not long survive unrevised, though the tendency of the reformed churches to fragment is a direct result of the overthrow of any belief in any divinely-assisted organ of authority. The appeals to private against corporate understanding of scripture look as if they were depending on a very clear and readily intelligible distinction. But is this really the case? Few people remain totally uninfluenced by the environment in which they were once educated and now live. We are not isolated units, totally private and independent of each other. And on the other hand, communities are composed of individuals, and if they belong to the Church they all possess in their own measure the gift of the indwelling Spirit. But when all this has been said and all allowances have been made for rapprochement, there is a residue even now of that over-sharp contrast that seems to have

54

begun with the Reformation.

Writing as late as 1962, an Anglican theologian maintained that the attempts made by Catholic scholars to defend the roles of authority or tradition in the formation of doctrine are misguided, if not dangerous. On these grounds he criticizes such writers as Congar and Tavard. He writes, and this is typical of his general method of approach:

> Though we certainly cannot rule out the possibility that the earliest version of the Gospel we can recover is, so to speak, a Church-shaped Gospel, Congar's assumption that this situation could and should continue indefinitely, indeed permanently, is an unwarrantable one. He can only make it by ignoring the significance of the formation of the Canon. In an attempt to do justice to one factor in the situation he ends by putting the whole possibility of revelation in jeopardy (R. P. C. Hanson, *Tradition in the Early Church*, p. 240).

We have already seen how open to objection it is to assert that the establishment of the canon did in fact stop further development. But Hanson's approach has the added disadvantage of failing to do adequate justice to the precise sense in which a Catholic holds the complementary value of tradition. Rather than being an independent source of information, it renders explicit what was already implicit in the written text of scripture. Hanson wants to be sure beforehand that the tradition is in accordance with the plain sense of scripture and finds himself unable to accept considerable tracts of tradition simply because they fail to conform to this very exacting standard. In other words, he wants to discern the meaning of what is earlier, and then in the light of the answer he arrives at he proposes to acquit or condemn what comes after. This effectually means that if the exegetical sense of scripture fails to support a meaning later than it, then that meaning is an unwarrantable corruption of the Gospel. No reasons, however, are produced to show why we should accept so very constricting a premise. Instead of interpreting the later by the earlier, what is to prevent us from adopting a more historical approach and interpreting the earlier by the later?

One of the most famous and typically Liberal-Protestant attempts to get back to the 'real message' by shearing away the accretions of centuries is to be found in the Hibbert Lectures of 1886 delivered by Edwin Hatch.

> It is impossible for anyone to fail to notice a difference of both form and content between the Sermon on the Mount and the Nicene Creed. The Sermon on the Mount is the promulgation of a new law of conduct: metaphysics are wholly absent. The Nicene Creed is a statement partly of historical facts, partly of dogmatic inferences; the metaphysical terms which it contains would probably have been unintelligible to the first disciples (*The Influence of Greek Thought on Christianity,* p. 1).

Nothing could be clearer, at least in intention. The book that follows is a development of the thesis that the change is the result of influences alien to the peculiar genius of Christianity. For Hatch, in effect, the post-resurrection Church becomes a historical phenomenon of exactly the same type as any other political or social organism. He introduces in a characteristically Protestant fashion a wedge between the essential nature of Christianity and the forms it assumes. It is the central commitment of the heart that is all-important in religion, the psychological conviction of salvation, or what Schleiermacher at the close of the eighteenth century was to call the religious feeling. The Modernists at the opening of this century were infected with much the same idea. And this approach has received its own tragic reversal. The very

56

book on which all was once built has proved to be unreliable quicksand. As the result of a process that culminated in the *Quest of the Historical Jesus* by Albert Schweitzer, the New Testament itself was subjected to a thorough process of historical and literary criticism and no generally acceptable conclusions have been arrived at. By removing religion from the sphere of dogma and sacrament to that of self-authenticating religious experience Luther appears to have been deeply influenced by the desire to justify his search for psychological assurance of his own salvation that appears to have dogged his steps from an early period. His influence succeeded in changing the meaning of faith from 'believing without doubting whatever God has revealed' to a deeply-felt conviction of the redeeming merits of Christ for me.

CHAPTER SIX

THE ORTHODOX APPROACH

> Personal prayer is possible only in the context of the community – nobody is a Christian by himself, but only as a member of the body. Even in solitude, 'in the chamber', a Christian prays as the member of a redeemed community, of the Church. And it is in the Church that he learns his devotional practice (G. Florovsky, *Private Prayer and Corporate,* p. 3).

It is this refusal to split up the Christian life into different compartments that is possibly the most valuable insight into the nature of the Church that Orthodoxy has to offer us. This belief in the unity of the Christian life springs from a very deep conviction of the all-pervasive action of the Holy Spirit. It is he above all who is active in the central activities, the central mysteries of the life of the Christian.

If we consider the main instances where the western habit of mind has succeeded in compartmentalising the life of the Church, the nature and (even more) the value of the Orthodox antidote will become all the more apparent. First, there is the gap between theology and religion or theology and prayer which is one of the more regrettable consequences of the introduction of the logical and scientific spirit into the study of theology. So much time has to be spent on the establishing of the correct texts and the meaning of words that the life-enriching value of the texts themselves tends to be pushed further and further into the background, and one can arrive at the situation that what is understood by theology can be and at times is carried on by men who are totally foreign to the spirit of the men whom they are interpreting. The

Eastern tradition would find such a situation intolerable. For them now, as it was for their ancestors, theology is the way to the understanding of the great mysteries of the Faith. It is the way of initiation that has as its object the direct and personal awareness of God; it must by its very nature end up in the direct speaking to God in prayer to which Evagrius of Pontus (d. 399) refers when he says, 'If you are a theologian you will pray in truth, and if you pray in truth you are a theologian' (PG 79.1180B). Such a spirit is a far cry from the anti-intellectual approach to the spiritual life that was and is a sad feature of much spiritual writing in the Western tradition, both reformed and Catholic.

Another distinction that the Orthodox are unwilling to draw is that between private and public prayer. It is the very obvious break between the community and the individual, between corporate and individual prayer that the Western liturgical movement tries to overcome. The Eastern Church never seems to have felt the need of such a renewal. You are never only a private individual with your own private conscience either for purposes of prayer or for purposes of belief. And this insight again is a product of the doctrine of the Holy Spirit, who because he informs all the Church all the time cannot be considered as restricting himself to any particular person or point of time. And it is this that gives the Orthodox such an immense respect for the principal paths that the Holy Spirit has trodden in the past.

The result of this approach has coloured the outlook of the Orthodox Church in a way that distinguishes her from the West. In contrast with the tendency of theology in the West to see problems in terms of conflicting ideas (e.g. conscience versus authority), Eastern thought tends to unify, and crystallizes round the ideas of Sobornost and Tradition. Both of these concepts are assertions of the unity of Christian experience against the disruptive forces that seek to separate the individual from the community and the present from the past.

Whereas Catholics have tended to look for the action of the Spirit in the voice of the teaching magisterium of the Church and Protestants in the voice of the individual conscience, Orthodox, especially those of the Russian tradition, tend to see the Spirit as acting through all the community. The word used by the Russians to describe this belief is 'Sobornost', a term meaning 'conciliarity'. The word is a relatively recent coinage and dates only to the last century. It expresses an attitude of mind which believes firmly in the corporate nature of worship and the need of charitable collaboration.

The other field in which the Orthodox belief in the action of the Spirit is evident is the conviction of the importance of the past in determining the beliefs of the present. The tendency to appeal to the past as a criterion of true belief is not new nor is it discreditable. Appeal to Scripture is one of the typical arguments of the writers of the second century, and later than that we find Athanasius quoting Origen and Theodoret quoting Athanasius. As early as the fifth century we find a considerable amount of activity being expended on the solid, useful, worthy and uninspiring task of compiling florilegia, that is collections of the sayings of the great men of the past. It is a moot point whether such industry is evidence of loss of confidence in the present and the need to appeal to the authority of the past in order to justify the beliefs of the present. So successful were the compilers that in at least one case their compilation was passed off as the original work of St Athanasius. So powerful was the influence of the past on the thinking of the present that St John of Damascus in the eighth century remarks in his treatise on the icons, 'We do not change the everlasting boundaries that our Fathers have set, but we keep the tradition just as we received it'. Such an attitude was not calculated to encourage confidence in the value of new thoughts and bold speculation. There has been in consequence a tendency to accept the findings of the past and not to reformulate in a new idiom. I say a 'tendency', because there have been distinguished theologians in the Greek church of whom this is not true. Simeon the New Theologian (949-1022) and Gregory Palamas (1296-1359) are great theologians by any standard. And now there is a considerable movement away from the over-tender clinging to the past which is really not in line with the other great Orthodox principle, the continued action of and presence with the Church of the Holy Spirit through all the ages.

CHAPTER SEVEN

NEWMAN AND THE DEVELOPMENT OF DOCTRINE

As a direct consequence of the hardening of positions that followed the close of the Reformation period, the difference between Catholics and Protestants came to be seen as that between those who drew their doctrines and practice from all the accumulated wisdom of the past and those who were content to rely on scripture alone. Both sides thought of the factors involved in too static terms: doctrines were established in the past and could not change. Catholics were eager to prove that their doctrines, if not scriptural, at least had the support of the ancient Fathers, bishops and doctors of Christ's Holy Catholic Church. In the period that comes between the close of the sixteenth and opening of the nineteenth centuries extensive careful researches were made into the historical basis of dogma with the avowedly apologetic aim of proving that Catholic doctrine was what it had always been, the faith of the early Church. It was an appeal to tradition, and it was of considerable importance to controversialists of both sides to show that their views of the Church and Christian doctrine had better claims to be regarded as antique than did those of their adversaries. When, therefore, towards the middle of the seventeenth century the French Jesuit Petavius dared to question the orthodoxy of the pre-Nicene Fathers it is easy to appreciate the hostility his work provoked. If he was correct, the appeal to tradition as a sure source of sound doctrine could no longer be allowed to pass unquestioned. When Bishop Bull, the Anglican controversialist, refuted or was thought to have refuted the damaging suggestions of Petavius, he was given a public vote of thanks by the Synod of French clergy. Bishop Bossuet also appealed to the continual traditions of the Fathers in order to prove the immutability of doctrine. These relatively small points are of some importance as they help to show both the background against which to assess the contribution made by Newman to the problem, and the firm conviction possessed by both sides in the debate that, whatever else dogmas might be, they did not develop. In this belief both sides were at one with a large body of patristic opinion. Irenaeus has no development, the Vincentian Canon effectively admits of none, the Council of Trent is silent.

Newman's own account of his progress towards a full acceptance of Catholic truth is traced in his reply to Charles Kingsley, the *Apologia pro Vita Sua*. His earliest convictions, derived from his parents and early education, were of a decidedly Calvinistic character. He was gradually weaned from this, especially by the history and writings of Thomas Scott, whose sayings, Newman claims, became almost proverbs. One of them was to have some importance in his own pilgrimage: 'Growth the only evidence of life.' He gradually moved away from the Calvinism of his youth, with its exclusive dependence upon faith and the Bible, and came to appreciate more and more the importance of tradition. He ascribes this particular stage in his conversion to a sermon he heard preached as an undergraduate by Dr Hawkins.

He lays down a proposition, self-evident as soon as stated, to those who have at all examined the structure of Scripture, viz. that the sacred text was never intended to teach doctrine, but only to prove it, and that, if we would learn the doctrine, we must have recourse to the formularies of the Church; for instance to the catechism and the creeds. He considers that after learning from them the doctrines of Christianity, the inquirer must verify them by Scripture (*Apologia*, chap. 1).

This is the classic Anglican doctrine, and on this theory tradition does little more than give formal expression to views already to be found in the New Testament. It does not really allow for growth and development, and, as we shall see, was the most prominent, if not the only, view in Newman's mind, until circumstances forced him to rethink his position.

This attitude to the past is closely connected with the appeal to antiquity, on which the attack on both Catholic and Calvinist arguments was based. Newman in common with the rest of the Tractarians maintained that the Church of England was a *via media* between the undesirable extremes of its two rivals. In order to substantiate such a claim they had to prove that the Anglican Communion was at one with the early Church in its beliefs. It laid, in particular, claim to the attribute of Antiquity. This is the reason for their return to the Fathers of the Church before the division of East and West. It is the reason for the *Library of the Fathers* begun about this time under the editorship of Newman. It is also the reason for the *Tracts for the Times*, which attempted to direct the eyes of the readers to various ancient liturgical practices and doctrinal beliefs that were in danger of being forgotten or neglected. A passage from the *Apologia* well illustrates the approach of the Oxford Movement.

These then are the parties in the controversy: – the Anglican Via Media and the popular religion of Rome. And next as to the issue, to which the controversy between them was to be brought, it was this: – the Anglican disputant took his stand upon antiquity or Apostolicity, the Roman upon Catholicity. The Anglican said to the Roman: 'There is but one faith, the ancient, and you have not kept it;' the Roman retorted: 'There is but one Church, the Catholic, and you are out of it.' The Anglican urged: 'Your special beliefs, practices, modes of action, are nowhere in Antiquity', etc.... the cause lay thus, Apostolicity versus Catholicity (*Apologia*, chap. 3).

It does not require much imagination to realise what Newman must have felt when his attempt to give a Catholic sense to the Anglican Thirty-Nine Articles of Religion was vehemently repudiated by the very men to whom he owned allegiance and whom he was also attempting to rescue from latent Calvinism and rationalism. *Tract XC* was condemned in 1841, and Newman retired to Littlemore. It was there that he wrote between 1841 and 1845 *An Essay on the Development of Christian Doctrine*. Nor was it a totally new idea. As we have seen, it had formed part of the background of his mind from a relatively early period in his life. In the *Apologia* he describes his mental state as follows:

Thus I am brought to the principle of development of doctrine in the Christian Church, to which I gave my mind at the end of 1842. I had made mention of it in the passage quoted many pages back, in 'Home Thoughts Abroad' published in 1836; and at an even earlier date I had introduced it into the History of the Arians in 1832; nor had I ever lost sight of it in my speculations (chap. 4).

Consideration of this feature of the Christian Church led him to the conclusion that 'modern Rome was in truth ancient Antioch, Alexandria, and Constantinople, just as a mathematical curve has its own law and expression'. He saw the Church as a developing organism possessed of a developing body of doctrines.

Development in the Church is a particular example of the more general problem and phenomenon of change. The Church is a living historical organism; therefore it is only natural that she also should change. But even granted the necessity of alteration, are there any laws for

65

determining whether or not the changing object remains true to type? Can history of itself provide us with a criterion for distinguishing between true and false developments? This is indeed a historical problem but not exclusively so. From the outset it is clear that truth and falsehood are not qualities that emerge from a purely dispassionate examination of the evidence. In order to answer the question at all you have to have some idea of the sort of answer you are looking for; in other words you need what Newman calls 'antecedent considerations'. If the ideal is objective history, such a procedure appears distressing. Whereas the inductive historical approach advocated by men like Lord Acton provides answers to no problems and contents itself with an accurate statement of the evidence and a view of both sides of the difficulty, the doctrinaire approach of many solutions does not commend itself.

This is precisely the objection made to Newman's method by Owen Chadwick in his book, *From Bossuet to Newman: The Idea of Doctrinal Development*. His central criticism is that Newman wants to solve a historical problem, the growth of the Christian Church, without keeping to a strictly historical method. Newman predefines by a sort of creative insight the qualities he expects in the Church of Christ. But such a criticism presupposes that there are only two methods of procedure; either you must beg the question or be content to abide by the rules of the game of scientific history. Chadwick makes no attempt to justify this axiom; and the suspicion remains that it is an effort to eliminate before the game begins a way of arguing that does not fit into the empirical strait-jacket. And it may be doubted whether Newman in the *Development* was setting himself a purely historical exercise. His argument is rather more subtle than the above critique allows for. It is neither purely logical nor purely historical. Neither his tory by itself nor logic by itself can prove that what did happen ought to have happened. Newman's great contribution to the whole debate is that he breaks away from the static approach to the problem of dogmatic truth that is at the basis of the previous attempts to defend the results of nearly two thousand years of Church history. Whereas Bossuet had said, 'We believe as we do because such has been the unchanging tradition of the Church', Newman says, 'Although there is a real continuity between the Church of the Fathers and the Church of 1865, you must not expect to find the same words being used all the time. Dogmas, like acorns and unlike family heirlooms, develop; therefore the principle of identity will be more difficult to identify'.

The second part of the *Development* is an attempt to provide an instrument with which to assess the truth or falsity, the rightness or wrongness of the varied changes that had come over the Church from the earliest days of her history. And here, in a sense, Newman was in a difficult position, as he was committed from the outset to defending the authenticity of the development of the doctrines held by the Church at the time of writing. The critical tool must at the same time be a defensive weapon: it is at the same time critical of what is outside the Church and apologetic of what is within. Further, it is very hard for Newman to point out any deviations by the Church in its past history, as admission of past defection has the effect of putting a question-mark at least beside the situation now arrived at. This is in fact one of the most serious drawbacks in the seven marks that Newman provides for distinguishing true and false developments; they tend to a justification of the *status quo*. It is a noble attempt to create what Solomon is recorded as having asked for at the opening of his reign: 'Give thy servant an understanding mind that I may discern between good and evil' (1 Kings 3.9). But the understanding is primarily retrospective; it is a way of looking at the past and justifying the present, rather than of assessing the value of a new movement. One of the examples he provides to show the unpredictability of past growth is the incident recorded in the tenth chapter of the Acts of the Apostles, where Peter is persuaded against his better judgement of the necessity of the mission to the Gentiles. To him at the time it did not appear a desirable step; it was out of keeping with all that he had thought that Christ was about. And Newman's seven marks would not have been much use in helping him to come to a decision.

The following are what he proposes. A true development is marked by preservation of type, continuity of principle, power of assimilation, logical sequence, anticipation of the future, conservative action on the past and chronic vigour. The illustration that Newman is fond of using is that of the living organism, the acorn growing into the oak or the child turning into the man. There is continuity and at the same time there is change. The body may alter outwardly while remaining the same or it may treacherously remain the same to look at while altering radically. So while in theory the British Constitution has altered little since the days of George III, the realities have changed much. But if the country were suddenly to adopt a republican form of government, the appearance would be greatly changed, but not the reality. The doctrines of the Church are similarly an organic whole developing in accordance with a set of principles which are, as it were, the life of the systems they create. Again like a living body they assimilate matter from the outside as the Church comes to greater self-consciousness and is able to define itself and its beliefs against the secular background. But it must always remain true to itself. True development is not a corruption, he maintains, in proportion as it seems to be a logical issue of what goes before. And with this mark it cannot be wrong to connect the belief that true development does not contradict or reverse the past. Definitions of the Church enhance and enlarge on the past rather than deny it. The Immaculate Conception, for instance, should give us a clearer awareness of the truth and meaning of the redemption wrought in and for us by Christ (cf. *Apologia*, chap. 5).

The analogy, as we have seen, is that of the developing organism. But it must in fairness be pointed out that at several points the analogy breaks down. The tree and the child are not really responsible for their way of physical growth. The Church has its future in its own hands. Again the path of a tree's growth is sufficiently obvious, we are quite clear about the contours of an oak, but we do not yet know what the Church will or ought to look like. Many would say now that one of the mistakes of the past was the attempt to ossify or fix the Church into an unchanging order and so to identify a particular structure with the Church. The simple fact is that we do not know with any degree of precision what the future holds in store. But perhaps the most unsatisfactory feature of Newman's treatment is the one already hinted at; that he has selected precisely those features that will end up with the conclusion that true development is to be found only within the Catholic Church. So in Chapter 12 of his book he has the following to say about the chronic vigour, which is the last of the seven marks.

When we consider the succession of ages during which the Catholic system has endured, the severity of the trials it has undergone, the sudden and wonderful changes without and within that have befallen it, the incessant mental activity and the intellectual gifts of its maintainers, the enthusiasm it has enkindled, the fury of the controversies that have been carried on among its professors..., it is quite inconceivable that it should not have been broken up and lost, were it a corruption of Christianity.

We almost feel ourselves back in the days of the old apologists for the faith of the first few centuries. The argument, shorn of the beauty of its style, simply runs: 'Look at the success of the Church and acknowledge its heavenly origin and mission'.

As soon as one begins to inspect a little more closely the implications of this more dynamic approach to the issue of doctrinal formation, the difficulty of applying this approach and the criteria offered becomes apparent. In other words, development is a key idea but needs careful handling. Even so, although we reduce what Newman has to say to three simple points – that the doctrines of the Church form an organic body; that therefore they form a growing body; that one must build on the past without being a slave to it – we have something. If we allow ourselves to be guided by this ideal we will be able to avoid the dangers of slavish subservience to the past and of uncritical acceptance of the novel. The Church, the Body of Christ, the People of God is ever being built up and on the way to the discovery of new and deeper awareness of the message once entrusted to the saints. The two principal hazards to be avoided are that the past has nothing or that the past has everything to tell us about the future. Here we have no perpetual dwelling-place; we are ever on the way to discover more of the truth.

But when all has been said, are we much further forward in the search for a measure for doctrine? All that can so far be said is that scripture is not the sole court of appeal, that living tradition is contained not only in the books of the Church, but also in the continuing experience of Christians, crystallized and authorized by the magisterium. As Newman argued in his essay *On Consulting the Faithful in Matters of Doctrine*, the ordinary believers may retain a firmer grasp of truth than bishops or theologians. The barely articulated instincts of believers may be a surer guide to sound doctrine than the reasons produced by them would lead one to suspect. In other words *legem credendi statuit lex orandi*: the way people pray determines what they believe.

Much of the discussion so far has been concerned with the way in which the Church as a result of various pressures has defended the conclusions and positions to which history has brought her. So Irenaeus defends the canon of scripture and the interpretation put upon it by the Church of his time by referring to the apostolic authority of the Church at Rome and the apostolic authorship of the gospels; Vincent of Lerins appeals to the constant teaching of the universal Church; and to the attack of the Reformers on all nonscriptural traditions the Council of Trent replies that scripture alone is inadequate. Newman's theory of development is meant partly to explain and partly to defend the action of the past upon the deposit of faith. All the criteria offered for defending the tradition of the Church are apologetic; that is, they defend what has actually happened by trying to prove that it ought to have happened. It is only in the fact of opposition from without or of criticism from within that the Church has seen the importance of justifying its past. The criteria it suggested are elements in its own history which act as a check upon it. In other words the purity or correctness of the tradition of the Church is maintained by making sure at least that it is not self-contradictory. What we believe now is consonant with, if not exactly the same in form as, what our fathers believed. But what is there to ensure that this is so? What is there to guard the deposit of faith? The most famous solution to this problem was provided by the First Vatican Council with its teaching on Papal Infallibility, and it is to that we now turn.

CHAPTER EIGHT

VATICAN I AND PAPAL INFALLIBILITY

The teaching of the First Vatican Council is yet another attempt to solve the problems of the criterion of doctrinal orthodoxy. When it assembled on the feast of the Immaculate Conception 1869, preparations had already been under way for over two years, as had ecclesiastical politics. There were present at the Council roughly three parties. First, there was a largish central party, that did not deny the infallibility of the Pope, but thought its definition inappropriate at that time. They are normally called 'Inopportunists', and contained in their number some of the most distinguished bishops of the period, notably Darboy of Paris and Dupanloup of Orleans. To the left of them were those who opposed the definition, and among them a few survivals of the old Gallican clergy, who asserted, in common with the Gallican Articles of 1682, that according to the decrees of the Council of Constance general councils had authority over the Pope. At Vatican I this view was represented by Mgr Maret, whose work *Du Concile Général et de la Paix Religieuse* appeared in 1869. The right wing, headed by Deschamps of Malines and organised by the redoubtable Manning of Westminster, were eager for a full definition of almost unlimited powers. They were known as the Ultramontanes. They acquired a majority on the Commission on Faith, and laboured with undisguised zeal for the furtherance of their cause. The fears of both sides and of the large central party are easy to understand. The Ultramontanes were for preserving the Church against the major enemies to religion of the time, rationalism, nationalism and liberalism, forces to which even Newman, an Inopportunist by temperament, was firmly opposed. The Inopportunist, on the other hand, feared, and not without good reason, some of the more extreme expressions of the Ultramontane view, which would make of every utterance of the Holy Father, public or private, an infallible pronouncement. Some such extreme view was held by Ward, the editor of the *Dublin Review*, Vaughan, the editor of the *Tablet*, and Veuillot, the editor of l'*Univers*, a violently pro-papal production. In his enthusiasm for his new-found faith Ward was quite prepared to accuse his opponents of disloyalty to the Holy See and formal heresy. His tendency was to treat the Pope as the subject of perpetual inspiration; he even claimed that 'infallible decisions were whispered into the Pope's ear by the Holy Spirit'. A dangerous ally for the Pope.

Had either of the extremes gained control of the proceedings at the council there would have been either no decision at all or one that greatly enlarged the scope of papal prerogative. More moderate counsels prevailed, as on previous occasions, and the final decree passed on 18th July, 1870 is a compromise solution. Papal infallibility is indeed defined, but the area in which it may operate is strictly limited to statements on faith and morals; and even in those fields only those definitions are infallible which the Pope makes when he speaks '*ex cathedra*', that is, as shepherd and teacher and ruler of all Christians. Not every pronouncement of the Holy Father requires the assent of faith. It was Bishop Gasser who set the minds of the large central party at rest by explaining on 11th July the limits to infallibility arising from the circumstances and the matter that is defined.

In the document that expresses the final mind of the Church, a short prehistory of the dogma is given, starting with the Fourth Council of Constantinople (869) and mentioning further Lyons II (1274) and Florence (1438-

45). Not that these are the earliest references to the Roman primacy, which was in a fairly flourishing state as early as the pontificate of Innocent I (402-417). But the *primacy* as then understood did not clearly imply the *infallibility* of the Pope. The scope of Papal infallibility is explicitly said in the Vatican definition to refer not to the discovery of new doctrines, but solely to the preservation and exposition of the deposit of faith (Dz 3070). The Pope is in the first place the preserver and outliner of the faith, not a creator of new dimensions. If he exceeds the fairly constricting limits put upon him, the ensuing pronouncement lacks the quality of infallibility. If, for example, the Pope spoke on some new scientific discovery, though what he said would merit respect, it would not have any particular weight over and above the actual arguments employed. The wording of the decree is as follows:

> The Roman Pontiff, when he speaks *ex cathedra*, that is, when in virtue of his supreme apostolic authority he uses his office of Shepherd and Teacher of all Christians to define a doctrine of faith or morals to be held by the whole Church, as a result of the divine assistance promised to him in Blessed Peter, possesses that infallibility with which our divine Redeemer wished the Church to be equipped for defining doctrines of faith or morals. Therefore definitions of the Roman Pontiff of that type, of themselves and not as a result of the consent of the Church, are irreformable (Dz 3074).

The final sentence was inserted to oppose the Gallican tendency of making the infallible nature of *ex cathedra* pronouncements depend on the approval of the faithful. Such a careful delimiting of papal claims should allay the fears of those who suspect that infallibility crushes all freedom of thought. There has been only one clear example of the use of this form of authority since the

74

promulgation of 1870: the dogma of the Assumption defined in 1950.

One of the main effects of the definition of 1870 has been to pinpoint the spheres where infallibility operates and the particular occasions within that area where un-hesitating assent must be given. As a result it has been too readily supposed that outside the particular instances mentioned the rest is unimportant; non-infallible utteran-ces can be safely ignored. Instead of being regarded as a help to the following of Christ, infallibility is therefore looked on as an infringement of liberty to be disregarded as often as it is not mortally sinful to do so. It is the same sort of attitude as is found towards the Mass among those who say that all that really matters are the words of consecration; there remain other parts indeed, but these could be omitted without loss. So too by pinpointing several special areas of competence for papal authority to work in, all other areas are automatically downgraded, non-*ex cathedra* pronouncements of the pope are said to be not binding and episcopal statements are conveniently bypassed.

One of the most serious criticisms of the decree of Vatican I is precisely this, that it exalts the authority of the Pope to the detriment of the bishops. They appear almost as mere delegates or representatives of the Pope. And that was exactly what Dupanloup, Hefele and others feared and predicted would happen well before the First Vatican Council opened. But the somewhat unbalanced picture that emerged was in large measure due to the outbreak of the Franco-Prussian war in the autumn of 1870. The Council was disbanded before its business was half over and did not reassemble. The intention to define the 'infallibility with which our divine Redeemer wished the Church to be equipped' could not be carried out. The consequence was that the absolute, personal, separate character of papal claims came to be over-emphasised, while the collegial, corporate nature of the episcopate was forgotten, only to be gloriously resurrected ninety years later at the Second Council of the Vatican. There we read, to anticipate a little, in the *Constitution on the Church*, that as Christ founded a college of apostles, so now there exists a similar body, a college of bishops, the joint weight of whose powers is larger than the sum of the parts. The existence of this college, however, requires that the pope be accepted as its head. The Constitution goes on explicitly to assert that the Pope still retains alone full authority over the Church. It looks very much as if Vatican II were trying to have it both ways by asserting that the Church is an absolute and constitutional monarchy at the same time. There seem, in other words, to be two sources of authority, the Pope by himself and the Pope together with the college of bishops. Possibly the very untidiness of this solution reflects the untidiness of the New Testament, where the college of the apostles and St Peter appear to receive equal powers (cf. Mt 16.18; 18.18; Lk 22.28-32). Some modern theologians, however, such as K. Rahner and Bishop B. C. Butler, clear up the untidiness by maintaining that when the Pope exercises authority over the Church, he always does so as head of the college; even when he acts alone, he does so not

as a 'private person' but as visible head of the Church, which the Pope is only when he is a member of the Church, living from its Spirit and from the institution as a whole. If he has to act as visible head of the Church, then he has to act as head of the college (K. Rahner in *Commentary on the Documents of Vatican II*, ed. H. Vorgrimler, Burns & Oates – Herder, 1967, I.204).

The Pope's act [in pronouncing infallibly] stems from the revealed faith of the infallible Church, a revelation which the Pope will in fact always fol-

76

low... by virtue of the assistance of the Holy Spirit... Hence too the *ex cathedra* definitions of the Pope can never lack the assent of the believing Church (*ibid.*, p. 213).

However, even the infallibility of the Pope, from which so much was hoped and feared, has not provided the Church with the neat tool for solving its difficulties that Ward and Manning so confidently expected. Its clear use has been rare indeed. There exist, for example, varying estimates of the authoritative character of *Humanae Vitae* (1968) and of Leo XIII's bull *Apostolicae Curae* on Anglican orders (1896). To some these decrees and others like them possess the full irreformable status of infallible pronouncements; to others they do not close the door upon further discussion and investigation. To some they are inspired documents with the seal of Christ's authority on them; to others they are indeed to be reckoned with but are not the final answer, nor are they necessarily binding in conscience.

But if there appear to be no generally agreed criteria for deciding which documents are infallible and which are not, how are we helped by Vatican I? Negatively we are helped if we can get out of the way of asking with too much insistence the question, 'Is this particular decree infallible in the strict sense?' (We may learn as well to grow out of the rather crude mentality which asks of any action, 'Is this a mortal sin?') But the more positive effect of the definition has been to assert the principle of authority in the central concerns of human life. It is an attempt to proclaim the requirements of a divine society against what Newman calls 'the all-corroding, all-dissolving scepticism of the intellect in religious enquiries.' This it does by maintaining that there exists upon earth a society that is not solely of this world, but possesses in its head and members the power to speak for God himself.

In addition to its major pronouncements on the authority of the Pope in matters of faith and morals, Vatican I has also something to say on the relation between scripture and tradition. The tendency to regard them as static, watertight compartments had not yet been much affected by Newman's *Development*, and the familiar wording of the Tridentine decrees is still easily discernible, though the terms are perhaps used more rigidly than at Trent. This constitution is in fact far nearer in ethos to Trent than it is to its opposite number in Vatican II. The section dealing with the appropriate roles of scripture and tradition, though headed, significantly enough, *Fontes Revelationis* (the Sources of Revelation), is little more than an exact word-by-word reproduction of Trent on the subject (Dz 3006).

Its view of the way in which the revelation has been handed on is expounded later in the same decree (Dz 3020). There it is noted that the deposit of faith is not like a philosophical discovery, which may be improved by the activity of mind upon it. Rather, the Council asserts, is it a precious treasure to be entrusted to future generations and carefully preserved by the present one. The Church's primary duty is to keep it faithfully and proclaim it infallibly. The meaning which the Church has once given to the revelation of God in Christ must never be sacrificed in the name of greater understanding. So far it is the immutability of Christian doctrine that is being stressed. The passage closes, however, with a lengthy quotation from the *Commonitorium Primum* of Vincent of Lerins (ch. 23). This begins with an exhortation for the faithful to amplify the deposit by their learning and wisdom, but only as far as their position allows them and without departing from the sense and meaning of the original deposit. Vincent seems, in fact, to be taking away with one hand what he has just granted with the other.

This, as we have seen, is a recurrent difficulty. Can a

passage, one wants to know, have a meaning that is independent of its understanding? Can the understanding improve while the meaning remains unaltered? Here can be seen the tension between the idea of revelation as a progress in awareness of the central mystery of Christ, an essentially dynamic approach, on the one hand; and on the other, revelation as a set of propositions to be found in the past history and documents of Christianity. Revelation was in a sense complete with the departure of Christ at his Ascension, and yet it is not complete until it has been accepted and understood by all those for whom it was intended from the beginning. So also salvation was achieved once and for all on Calvary and at the Resurrection, and yet we are still being saved. It is the familiar tension between the already and the not yet that we also meet in the life of Christ. At the end of the last book of the Bible we have the same idea expressed, 'I am the Alpha and the Omega, the first and the last, the beginning and the end' (Apoc 22.13). Right through the gospels the Kingdom of God is set inconsistently in the present and in the future, is said to be in this world and yet not of it. A similar tension is discernible in St Paul's writings. He is uncertain whether spiritual worship and justification require works or not, whether traditional morality has been set aside by the gospel or not, whether the spirit and the letter are opposed one to another or complement each other. In fact, the letter of the New Testament and the various traditions contained in the liturgy and the Fathers are expressions of the Spirit as he gradually explains to the Church the full meaning of Christ. But the letter is never either the same as the Spirit, nor totally separate from it. It is only when the Spirit comes to perfect expression in Christ, that the two are inseparable. Revelation will only be total with the dawn of the new creation so confidently expected by St Paul in his letter to the Romans:

For the creation waits with eager longing for the revealing of the sons of God; for the creation was subjected to futility, not of its own will but by the will of him who subjected it in hope; because the creation itself will be set free from its bondage to decay and obtain the glorious liberty of the sons of God (Rom 8.19-21).

CHAPTER NINE

VATICAN II

The First Vatican Council did little more than repeat the formula of Trent on scripture and tradition, apparently uninfluenced by the views of Newman on the development of doctrine. It upheld also the traditional views of the Church on the two sources of revelation. These two positions are, as we have seen, closely connected with a somewhat static idea of Christian doctrine, with a strong emphasis on the total adequacy of formulations already arrived at. It is as though the Church had already achieved perfection both in her structures and her formulas. If this is indeed true and the Church on earth is a perfect society, it follows both that no improvement is possible and that all change is sacrilege. This complex of attitudes and beliefs will in future, but with no unfavourable overtones, be called the 'conservative' view, the supporters of which at the opening of the council had tried to prejudge the issue precisely on the subject of revelation, by heading the initial draft of the decree 'On the two sources of revelation'. The opposition to this logically coherent position came from a body loosely termed 'progressives'. Again the expression is purely descriptive; it is intended to describe those who felt a certain unrest with the conservative view, without necessarily implying a coherent counterposition.

One of the interesting features of the post-Vatican II era is the disappearance of any neat system to replace or counter the old. Whatever the defects of the old vision of the Church – and there were many – it was at least clear and coherent; it showed you what must be done and believed if you wished to remain a Catholic. But now the position, though freer and less constricting, is different. It is harder to have to acknowledge that one may be wrong than to be content with a certainty imposed from above. The more tolerant and liberal attitude adopted by the Church at the Council does not condemn outright the conservative position; rather it denies to it the role of being *the* only view that a Catholic might hold. The conservative position on tradition, for example, becomes one among several possible positions; previously it had been the official Catholic line.

The main aim of the more progressive party was to restore to something like its correct position in the life of the Church the word of God in scripture. Their initial protest against the first draft of the *Constitution on Revelation* and the demand for a return to a scripture-centred approach imply an acceptance of some of the ideas of the Reformation. Here too is the view we have already seen put forward by Hawkins that the doctrines of Christianity must be verified by scripture. One of the most distinguished representatives of this movement back to the scriptures was the Jesuit Karl Rahner. The liturgical life of the Church has benefited enormously from this new stress, and the last chapter of the *Constitution on Revelation* deals with the use of the scriptures in the life of the Church. Inevitably this new stress has provoked a certain amount of opposition, particularly among those who regard it as a complete sell-out to the Reformation; and although it is not true that non-scriptural traditions have been rejected, the very introduction of so much scripture means a change of emphasis. In fact the abundant use of scripture in the text of the decree is one of its most refreshing aspects.

The second draft of *Dei Verbum*, the *Dogmatic Constitution on Revelation*, was debated from 30 September 1964 to 2 October. The resulting document was finally promulgated on 18th November of the next year by

Paul VI. It reflects the various tensions of which we have spoken, and is a very carefully balanced piece of work. It will be noted that to the familiar questions of the past no deceptively simple solutions are supplied. It is made up of a short prologue and six chapters. The first chapter deals with revelation itself, the second with its transmission, the third with the interpretation and inspiration of scripture, the fourth with the Old and the fifth with the New Testament, and the last with scripture in the life of the Church. It is interesting and important to note that, of the six chapters, four are concerned with scripture. Could more conclusive evidence be provided of the change in emphasis above referred to? Nor is this new look confined to passages of exhortation to the faithful. The text is a mosaic of scriptural quotations right the way through. The preface is half accounted for by a longish quotation from the beginning of the First Epistle of St John, and the ensuing chapter is either direct repetition or clear echo of the New Testament. The particular problem of tradition in all its various senses is tackled in the second chapter, to which we now turn.

Its main aim is to outline the principal ways in which the revelation of God in Christ has been handed down and is now available to us. The handing on of revelation is tradition; that is, the tradition is in the first place the action of handing on and only in a derivative sense what is handed on, the content of tradition; in addition there is a third meaning, namely, what is handed down but is not in scripture, and this third group again subdivides into ancient and apostolic traditions and ecclesiastical traditions. Part of the confusion of the previous debate had arisen from the failure to distinguish the last two kinds of tradition. These distinctions are not explicitly made in the decree despite requests that they should be, and an atmosphere of imprecision pervades the constitution as a result.

The second chapter sets itself to answer the question with which this book opened:

> In his gracious goodness, God has seen to it that what he had revealed for the salvation of all nations would abide perpetually in its full integrity and be handed on to all generations. Therefore Christ the Lord, in whom the full revelation of the supreme God is brought to completion (2 Cor 1.20; 3.16; 4.16), commissioned the apostles to preach that gospel which is the source of all living truth and moral teaching, and thus to impart them divine gifts (sect. 7).

The point is that the divine self-disclosure, in order to be effective, must become part of men's minds. It must be preached, listened to, absorbed and lived out. Faith requires a knowledge of its object if it is to exist at all. Commitment cannot be made in a vacuum. So St Paul writes to the Romans:

> But how are men to call upon him in whom they have not believed? And how are they to believe in him of whom they have never heard? And how are they to hear without a preacher? (Rom. 10.14).

It was by preaching in the first place that the message of salvation was handed down by Christ to the apostles and then in obedience to the command of the Lord to those that came after. But if the primary means of transmission is clear, what of the content? In the synoptic gospels it is the arrival of the Kingdom of God and the need of repentance that occupy the foreground; in the Fourth Gospel it is the person of Christ as saviour of the world. These are the varied traditions that lie behind the written text we possess. The period of merely oral preaching and tradition did not last indefinitely. The preaching carried on, but some of the teaching of Christ was written down, partly, at any rate, to provide a reliable record of what had happened. The dangers of distortion grew as the resurrection faded away into the past and the purity of the original Gospel was threatened. Inevitably, as St John notes at the close of the Fourth Gospel, the written account was not an exhaustive catalogue of the doings and sayings of Christ. Nor does the New Testament present us with revelation without comment. The four gospels are a sign, not the equivalent, of the Gospel.

The New Testament, then, contains revelation, but in two senses is not equivalent to it. First, the active role of preaching the gospel continued after the writing of the New Testament. The commission to preach did not immediately cease once the books of the Church had appeared.

> And so the apostolic preaching, which is preserved
> in a special way in the inspired books, was to be
> preserved by a continuous succession of preachers
> to the end of time (chap. 1, sect. 8).

Secondly, the living tradition is wider in scope than the New Testament, though the document still does not explain the sense in which this is true. Whether tradition preserves some truths of revelation which are not found in scripture, or simply deepens and clarifies the meaning of scripture, is left undecided.

> This sacred tradition, therefore, and sacred scripture
> of both the Old and the New Testament are like a
> mirror in which the pilgrim Church on earth looks at
> God (chap. 2, sect. 7).

Scripture is clearly not the same as living tradition, but can they be treated separately? As we have seen, the prevalent view since the Council of Trent has been that they can and that some revealed truths may be gathered from tradition alone. The only real question then was whether all traditions were equally valid or only apostolic traditions could be used as a source of revelation. Before Vatican II, however, the whole question was reopened and a strong minority thought that a far greater emphasis should be laid on the scriptures as the primary source of doctrine with tradition acting merely as confirmatory evidence where scripture needed it. The debates to which these conflicting views gave rise persuaded the Fathers that the wisest course was to decide the question neither way, but to state both sides of the problem and to leave the matter there. Section 8, therefore, limits itself to describing the two main ways in which revelation comes to us, namely scripture and tradition; while the ninth section insists on their unity of aim, origin and function:

> Hence there exist a close connection and communication between sacred tradition and sacred scripture. For both of them, flowing from the same divine wellspring, in a certain way merge into a unity and tend toward the same end (chap. 2, sect. 9).

At the beginning of the next section we have similarly,

> Sacred tradition and sacred scripture form one sacred deposit of the word of God, which is committed to the Church.

These passages give some idea of the way the Church wishes us to imagine the relationship between the various elements from which we draw our understanding of the gospel of Christ in its entirety. The growing awareness of the impact of our Lord upon the lives of the faithful is achieved by means of preaching, contemplation, study and prayer. No reference is made here to exegetical techniques as a way of arriving at this deeper understanding, possibly because there is a constant danger of forgetting that the appreciation of the full meaning of the gospel is not readily found outside the setting of the Church. This is an important point and is well illustrated by a passage in Newman's *Apologia*.

> The peculiarity of the Anglican theology was this, – that it supposed the truth to be entirely objective and detached, not (as in the theology of Rome) lying hid in the bosom of the Church as if one with

86

her, clinging to and (as it were) lost in her embrace
(chap. 3).

The truth that Newman saw about the Catholic Church
should never be forgotten, that the understanding of the
message of Christ can never be arrived at in isolation
from the teaching and practice of the Church, past and
present. It is self-defeating to cut oneself off from one's
past or to sidestep the history of the Church in order to
understand the books of the Church. Revelation is barely
separable from the effect it produces and the ripples it
sends out are part of the message it has for each of us.
This almost self-conscious stress on the Church as the
receiver and interpreter of the good news is a new accent
in the history of tradition. The Holy Spirit speaks to and
through the listening assembly of the faithful. It is in this
way that tradition is kept alive in the Church. The past is
continually being poured into and remoulded by the life
of the present.

The very complex nature of the way in which our
knowledge of revelation has reached us is by now apparent, and no attempt is made to adjudicate among the
different elements. All deserve respect, and at the close
of section 9 the decree contents itself with repeating unaltered the formula of Trent and Vatican I.

> Consequently it is not from sacred scripture alone
> that the Church draws her certainty about every-
> thing that has been revealed. Therefore both sacred
> tradition and sacred scripture are to be accepted and
> venerated with the same sense of devotion and
> reverence.

This is a very carefully worded formula and was added at
a fairly late date, as a result of a request from the Pope
himself. Behind it lies the debate already described between conservatives and progressives on the particular
sense in which scripture is sufficient for bringing us to a
full knowledge of revelation.

87

The Church is not external to the process she is responsible for carrying on; her function is not limited to passive reception of the word and faithful transmission. The Gospel is not like some classical text, nor is the main duty of Christian witness the discovery of the exact text and meaning of the New Testament. This point cannot be stressed too strongly: Christianity is an encounter with a person who is met in the Bible, in the assembly of the people of God and in the other writings and liturgy of the Church. In the words of the official drafting committee, whose comments represent the interpretation which was offered to the Council Fathers and was therefore presumably accepted by them, 'Neither is tradition presented as a quantitative complement of scripture nor is scripture regarded as an exhaustive codification of revelation'.

But what authority is to decide the correct sense of the message? And how is this authority related to the features it seeks to interpret?

> The task of authentically interpreting the word of God, whether written or handed on, has been entrusted exclusively to the living teaching office (*magisterium*) of the Church, whose authority is exercised in the name of Jesus Christ (chap. 2, sect. 10).

The teaching office of the Church is exercised by its bishops, not indeed in isolation from the rest of the Church – it is not as though the Holy Spirit spoke only through those in authority. At baptism all believers are ordained as sharers in the role of Christ as Prophet, Priest and King. So St John writes,

> But you have been anointed by the Holy One, and you all know... But the anointing you received from him abides in you and you have no need that anyone should teach you (1 Jn 2.20, 27).

And St Peter: 'But you are a chosen race, a royal priesthood, a holy nation, God's own people' (1 Pet 2.9). But

88

although the whole Church presents Christ to men, it is clear that within the single society there is a differentiation and that this was intended by our Lord. There is the special vocation of the apostles (Lk 6.13 ff.), there is the commission to celebrate the Eucharist (1 Cor 11.25), to preach (Mt 28.19), and to forgive sins (Jn 20.23; Mt 18.18). This authority was passed on to the bishops, and to these bishops in consequence the same sort of obedient submission is due as to the first apostles; not an unquestioning acceptance of everything but a predisposition to accept the decision of one who in a special sense represents Christ for us.

The fear of the Reformation that this type of authority weakened the power of scripture is to some extent allayed by the limits placed on the magisterium.

> This teaching office is not above the word of God but serves it, teaching only what has been handed on, listening to it devoutly, guarding it scrupulously and explaining it faithfully by divine commission and with the help of the Holy Spirit (chap. 2, sect. 10).

Reassuring though this may appear, it does not solve any problems, either about the respective roles of scripture, tradition and the magisterium or about the connection between the infallibility of the Church as reflected in the *sensus fidelium* (the general judgment of the spirit-filled faithful) and the infallibility of the magisterium of the pope and bishops. The latter point has already been dealt with and additional material may be found in section 25 of the *Constitution on the Church*; section 12 of the same decree deals with the inerrancy of the people of God. But the living relationship of dialogue, which is required if tradition is to be properly understood, cannot be easily reduced to rule.

The same is equally true of the problem of the roles of scripture, tradition and magisterium. *Solvitur ambulando;*

only by living through the difficulty can a solution be reached. Two Protestant commentators on the decree, Prior Roger Schutz and Frère Max Thurian, Reformed Monks of Taizé, who were the guests of the Council throughout its sessions, write as follows: –

Without scripture, tradition cannot know its true apostolic content; without the magisterium, tradition cannot be sure of being the true tradition of the Church, which began with the apostles, for want of an authentic interpreter to distinguish between faithful transmission of the Word of God and purely ecclesiastical traditions...

EPILOGUE

The Spirit was promised by Christ to the Apostles to guide them, and with them the Church over which they were set, into all truth (Jn 16.13). He is above all active in handing on to generations to come the message of salvation. But he works through the Church, which is the secondary agent in carrying on the good news, both preserving and interpreting it. To the voice of the Spirit all must be attentive listeners as he addresses us in scripture, tradition and the magisterium. No portion of his message must be neglected by those who seriously desire to worship him in 'spirit and truth' (Jn 4.24).

SUGGESTED FURTHER READING

General
M. J. Congar: *Tradition and Traditions* (Burns and Oates, 1966) – a very comprehensive and exhaustive study of the history of the problem; pre-conciliar in time but not in spirit.

Particular
On the New Testament and the Fathers:
J. N. D. Kelly: *Early Christian Doctrines* (4th ed. Black 1968) – extremely clear and balanced.
R. P. C. Hanson: *Tradition in the Early Church* (S.C.M. Press 1962) – adopts a very historical approach.

The Reformation
J. R. Geiselmann: *The Meaning of Tradition* (Burns and Oates 1966, p. 6) – contains a discussion of the meaning of Trent.

Newman
J. H. Newman: *The Development of Christian Doctrine* (Longman 1878, 2nd ed.)

Vatican II
G. Tavard: *Translation and Commentary on the Dogmatic Constitution on Divine Revelation of Vatican II* (Darton, Longman and Todd, 1966).
K. Rahner and J. Ratzinger: *Revelation and Tradition* (Burns and Oates, 1966).

INDEX

THEOLOGY TODAY SERIES

The following numbers have already been published:

The following numbers will be published in 1971:

First published in the Netherlands
Made and printed by Van Boekhoven-Bosch N.V. - Utrecht.